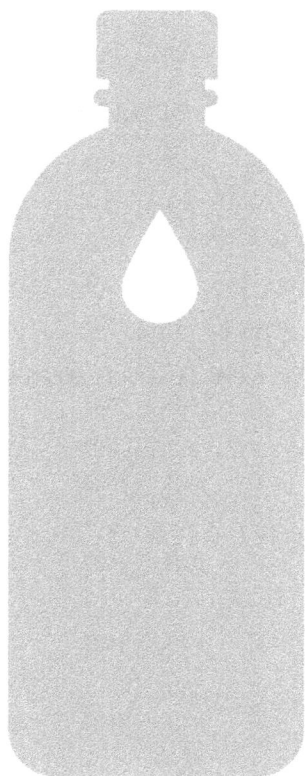

SIGNIFICANCETAB EDWARDS

ALSO BY TAB EDWARDS

Imperfekt

The Art of Movement

Doing Your Job Successfully

Management By Initiatives

The 50-Hour Workweek in 20 Hours

"

NOTHING IS PERFECT. LIFE IS MESSY.
RELATIONSHIPS ARE COMPLEX.
OUTCOMES ARE UNCERTAIN.
PEOPLE ARE IRRATIONAL."

HUGH MACKAY—
AUTHOR

"

THERE IS NO SUCH THING AS AN INSIGNIFICANT LIFE, ONLY THE INSIGNIFICANCE OF MIND THAT REFUSES TO GRASP THE IMPLICATIONS."

LAURENCE OVERMIRE—
AUTHOR, POET

SIGNIFICANCE

**A postulate of everyday irrational human behavior;
by otherwise rational human beings**

TAB EDWARDS

THE PERFORMANCE LABORATORY No 33 / TMBE MEDIA
PHILADELPHIA, PA. 19129

PHILADELPHIA, PA 19129

THE PERFORMANCE LABORATORY Nº 33 / TMBE MEDIA

ISBN 979-8-218-00309-8

This publication is designed to provide authoritative information in regards to the subject matter covered. It is sold with the understanding that the publisher is not engaged in rendering legal, accounting, or other professional services. If legal advice or other expert assistance is required, the services of a competent professional person should be sought.

–From a declaration of principles jointly adopted by a committee of the American Bar Association and a committee of publishers.

Tab Edwards books are available at special quantity discounts to use as premiums and promotions, or for use in corporate training programs. For more information, please contact us at Info@TheLab33.com.

www.TabEdwards.com/significance
Designed by Water Creative
Philadelphia, PA.

1   3   5   7   9   10   8   6   4   2

TTX

CONTENTS

CONTENTS

PART ONE

MOTIVATED BEHAVIOR

STAY WARM

At dawn, when you have trouble getting out of bed, tell yourself: 'I have to go to work—as a human being. What do I have to complain of, if I'm going to do what I was born for-the things which I was brought into the world to do? Or is this what I was created for? To huddle under the blankets and stay warm?"

-MARCUS AURELIUS-
ROMAN EMPEROR AND PHILOSOPHER

WHAT'S THE POINT? OR IS THERE ONE?

I have always been inquisitive. From an early age, I recall being curious about things like: How does Santa Clause get to *every* house in the world in *one* night? We don't even have a chimney, so how does he get into *our* tiny apartment? Why are my sisters' shirt buttons on the left side? What's the difference between an ocean and a sea? Why do people from different countries speak different languages? We learned about The Tower of Babel story, but it didn't make sense to me. If God wanted to stop the Babylonians from building a city, couldn't God just zap and destroy it, rather than stopping it by making people speak different languages so they couldn't understand each other? It seemed awfully inefficient. Why are our fingers different sizes? And: What flavor is *bubble gum*? It's not lemon, grape, or cherry, so what flavor *is* it?

As I got older, the curiosity didn't slow down: Why do people brag about getting "soooo drunk?" I thought people bragged about things that hardly anyone else could do. *Anybody* can get drunk. Why do old men and those seeking prestige and acceptance brag about playing golf? Did I just answer my own question? Why can't God defeat Satan? What age do you become when you get into heaven? If you die when you are 100 years old, do you go to heaven and live eternally as a wrinkly old man or woman? That would suck. Of all the Gods I learned about in school, why did my family choose Jesus's father and not Thor? I really liked Thor's Saturday morning cartoon when I was a kid. If people's lives go on exactly the same without an appendix as with one, then why do we have one in the first place? And a question that baffles us all: If we were created by a God, why did it create us?

The opening witticism by Marcus Aurelius, although humorous, embodies the ambiguity of existential questions about man's existence; why are we here? What is the meaning of our existence? What is our purpose in life? Is our purpose something that has been divinely inspired and instructed in religious scriptures (per Aurelius: "... the things which I was brought into the world to do")? Is it something that people can define by themselves for themselves ("... huddle under the blankets and stay warm")? Or do we have—or *need*—a purpose in life at all?

If there exists a *definitive* purpose for human existence, our pursuit of that purpose would motivate our
behavior toward achieving it, giving human beings
something definitive to aspire and work toward. How-
ever, if there is *not* a definitive *raison d'être* or life purpose,
then what motivates human behavior? Specifically,
what motivates the everyday *irrational* behavior of otherwise rational human beings?

By "everyday" human behavior, I am referring to behaviors which most—if not all—rational human beings
exhibit daily. For example, hating the new girl in school
because one sees her as competition for the boys' attention is an example of everyday irrational human behavior. It is irrational because it is senseless, serving no con-
structive purpose other than rationalizing the hater's
insecurities and making her feel artificially good about
herself. Another, weightier example of everyday irrational behavior is *racism*, which will be explored in greater
detail in a subsequent chapter. If there is a definitive
preordained purpose for human existence, what is it
within that purpose that motivates one group of people
to hate another just because they look different?

Any discussion about *purpose*, given the ambiguity
and disparity surrounding the topic, requires that we
establish a framework defining what we mean by "purpose," to facilitate a meaningful discussion about the
topic and its relationship to human behavior.

"Purpose" is generally defined as the reason why
something is done, created, or *for which something exists.*

Theologically and philosophically, however, purpose—as it relates to human life—can take on drastically different and more complex definitions. Theologically, life's purpose mostly relates to some form of divine salvation, gaining eternal life, or realizing spiritual enlightenment, transcending human consciousness. Philosophically, the concept of purpose is multifaceted and dissenting.

Prominent philosophers and acknowledged great thinkers have put forth answers to the question of life's meaning and our purpose on earth. Though the terminology used to describe *meaning* and *purpose* may differ from the way we refer to these concepts today, their theories are nonetheless worthy of consideration and invaluable to the discussion.

German philosopher Immanuel Kant wrote about the *highest good*; Friedrich Nietzsche—often associated with *Nihilism*—believed that life has no meaning *or* value (since God's "death"). Plato believed that the meaning of life is in attaining the highest form of knowledge of the *substance* of things from which objects and matter derive utility and value, the "Form of Good." But the philosopher whose writings provide what I consider the most useful insight into life's purpose was the Greek philosopher Aristotle.

In Aristotle's *Nicomachean Ethics*, he wrote that there is not a single determinant by which all things are good. He discussed his notion of human good or *eudaimonia*, which connotes success, well-being, and fulfillment, and is best translated as "happiness." Aristotle believed that happiness is the highest good because human beings can choose happiness as an end in and of itself. However, he believed that happiness is an activity and *not* an end state. **Virtue**, according to Aristotle, is a state of being; possessing the right virtues disposes a person to live well, and happiness is the activity of living well. He identified twelve virtues—character traits that make a "good" person—including friendliness, truthfulness, modesty, ambition, and other related characteristics.

Aristotle also believed that human beings have a **telos,** a Greek term referring to full potential or inherent purpose, which is similar to the notion of a goal or true function. He argued that human beings are "rational animals," and the human ability to reason and to *act on reason* is what separates us from other animals. Goodness, he believed, is achieved when a human being secures its telos. And since human beings have the ability to reason, we should pursue our telos—our **inherent purpose** or rationality. Therefore, he argues, our function in life is to realize our potential as rational beings.

"Our function in life is to realize our potential as rational beings"

-ARISTOTLE-

An Assumption of Rationality

If there is a preordained, divinely inspired, definitive reason why human beings exist and for what we are here to accomplish in our lifetimes, then any activity in which we engage that is in direct pursuit of achieving our life's goal would be *considered* rational behavior, even if the behavior is clearly irrational. The reason is that, theoretically, if one is operating from a code of behavior stated or guided by the divinely inspired words of theistic scriptures, then, by extension, their **related behaviors** must be considered rational to those who believe the scripture is divinely inspired. Even though such stated or divinely inspired behaviors may be seen as rational by followers of the instructive scriptures, to non-followers, the behaviors can be considered irrational, such as *dhabiha*, the Islamic method of slaughtering animals for halal (i.e., permissible) meats and poultry.

Halal food is the dietary standard prescribed in the Muslim scripture of the Qur'an. Muslims believe that all life, including those of animals, is sacred. Therefore, if an animal's life must be taken for human survival, it should be taken in the name of God. For food to qualify as halal, the animal must be well cared for, fed cleanly, and provided with access to water. At the time of slaughter, the name of Allah must be invoked, and the animal's face must be pointed toward Mecca. Then, with a sharp knife, the blade must slice across the animal's throat in one motion, to avoid undue stress for the animal. For Muslims, the dhabiha is considered a rational approach to taking the life of an animal for food. To animal-rights activists, the process is inhumane, because, however the process unfolds, in the end, one is still needlessly killing an animal for food, which they perceive as irrational.

As this example illustrates, even when one believes there is a preordained life mission, definitively known purpose, or reason for our existence, and behaviors are guided by and exhibited in accordance with scriptural teachings, behaviors can still be considered irrational by others with a different life paradigm or worldview. Following this premise, it is inevitable that *everyone* will engage in questionable, irrational, or even pathological behaviors at some point as we pursue both faith-based definitions of life's purpose and those we define for ourselves. It is the nature of being **free-willed**, which assumes we are in control of our own behavior and decisions—even for theists whose God is omniscient, omnipotent, and "has a plan for our lives"—and that conscious, reasoned thought determines our actions. We are human and, as humans, fallible.

There is an implicit assumption that we are all rational creatures, because of our humanness. Our upright posture, speech, and "rational" action—those based on or in accordance with **reason** or **logic**—are the chief characteristics of man, and what differentiates us from other mammals.

The term "rationality" can be value-laden as we use it in our everyday language, namely that "rational" thought or behavior is assumed to be good, whereas "irrational" thought or behavior is assumed to be bad, leading to negative outcomes. Rationality is a dual-process of thought, such as "rational" vs. "irrational," which ascribes a value to each term, or "controlled vs. automatic processing," for example, that focuses on the process of how people think. For my postulate, I will focus on the value-laden treatment of rationality, since, in our modern vernacular, we associate "rational" with good and "irrational" with problematic or bad. In this context, making decisions based on a "gut feeling" or emotion would be considered irrational, since the decision would not be based on reason or logic.

Is it rational to believe that there is a definitive purpose for human existence that has been defined by something or someone, yet, that same someone or something would not make it abundantly clear and unambiguous to all what that purpose is?

Do plants have a purpose? Does an aardvark have a purpose? If so, do we know this with certainty, or is it something that we believe makes sense based on ... something? Do we believe that plants and aardvarks know what their life's purpose is? Is it rational to believe such a thing? If not, then is it rational for human beings to believe that we have a pre-ordained purpose and know what it is, even though we are uncertain about its factual objectivity? I believe it is not.

In the scientific community, when a researcher offers a hypothesis for the cause or remedy of something, other scientists are often inclined to ask the researcher about their hypothesis, "Think, know, or prove?" Does the researcher *think* her hypothesis is correct, does she *know* that it is correct, and can she *prove* that it is correct? Until a hypothesis is provable, no one will believe that it is correct or fully baked. Do we *think* we know the factual reason why we exist? Many people *think* they do. Do we *know*, based on experience or certainty, the factual reason for our existence? No. Can we *prove* the factual reason for our existence? No. So, is it rational to live life *thinking*—with no proof—that [fill in a purpose] is the reason we live our lives and behave in a certain way, in hopes of fulfilling a purpose that we *think* is correct? I believe it is not.

Do We Even Need a Preordained, Definitive Purpose?

In his 2003 paper "Towards a cognitive theory of existential meaning," psychologist Jesse Bering suggests that humans are evolutionarily-compelled to find meaning and purpose in life. He writes:

> "A fourth, existential domain, an abstract ontological frame within which the subjective, narrative self is envisioned to be contained, may have driven the construction of an intuitive capacity in humans that encourages them to search for the underlying purpose or reason for having had certain life experiences."

Essentially, Bering theorizes that the need to construct meaning or purpose in life is a fundamental aspect of being human, and is not necessarily religious or philosophical. Expanding on this theme, neurologist and psychiatrist Viktor Frankl's theory of "Logotherapy" states that finding meaning and purpose in life is necessary for *happiness and well-being*. He asserts that it is the nature of human beings to search for life's purpose, which each individual **seeks and constructs for themselves**. Although Frankl's theory of Logotherapy, like Bering's theory, proposes that it is within *human* nature to seek out life's purpose, a drawback of Logotherapy, in my opinion, is its inability to separate nonreligious and religious motivations.

In her publication, "The Sources of Meaning and Meaning in Life Questionnaire (SoMe): Relations to demographics and well-being," Dr. Tatjana Schnell, a Professor at the Institute of Psychology, examines the shortcomings of popular measures of meaning in life, and how their use results in biased correlations between life meaning and well-being. Schnell concludes that meaningfulness can be a predictor of positive well-being, but is *not* predictive of negative well-being. This seems to neutralize Logotherapy's claim that finding meaning is *necessary* for well-being. That said, one thing on which all three researchers agree is that there is value in having meaning and purpose in life.

Research by Bering, Frankl, Schnell, and others are consistent in the notion that human beings need to construct meaning or purpose in life, for various reasons. However, it is worth considering if, as proposed by Bering, the quest for meaning or purpose is a fundamental aspect of being human—in other words, an **intrinsic human need**—or if it is born of natural human curiosity.

Human Curiosity

The subject of *curiosity* can be both complex and nuanced, such as why people *voluntarily* seek out curiosity (as opposed to it being omnipresent), situational determinants of curiosity, diversive versus trait curiosity, and other categorizations. My aim is to provide insight into whether or not human curiosity has an evolutionary or generally intrinsic basis—the underlying cause—to further the discussion of whether natural human curiosity could be a primary drive (intrinsic) for humans to seek out life's purpose, or a secondary drive (otherwise derived). If primary, then we can assume that every human being—whether religious or secular—will at some point be internally driven or compelled to wonder whether humans have a specific purpose for living, and what that purpose is.

Early discussions about curiosity saw it as an intrinsically motivated desire for information. Modern accounts interpret curiosity as an intrinsic, cognitively-induced *deprivation* that is borne of a deficit in knowledge or understanding. Aristotle, for example, believed that men studied science for intrinsic reasons, and not for practical or utilitarian ones. Cicero referred to curiosity as an innate love of knowledge. Both, however, acknowledged that there are also *extrinsic* motivators for curiosity.

In 1928, marine zoologist Walter Garstang developed a hypothesis called "The Garstang Hypothesis," about the metamorphosis of tadpole larva which, today, is referred to as *Neoteny*. Neoteny is an evolutionary short-cut which suggests that, as mature human beings, we retain juvenile characteristics, giving us an intrinsic child-like curiosity.

What becomes abundantly clear as we dig deeper into research on the cause and nature of curiosity and other information-seeking behaviors is that the source is ultimately unanswerable. We cannot definitely say that human beings seek answers to the question of life's meaning and purpose as a *fundamental condition of being human*: an evolutionary or generally intrinsic need to know such answers. Therefore, does our curiosity about life's purpose and ending mean that we *must have* such a purpose, or is it just that we *want to know* if there is such a purpose; and, if so, what it is? There are undoubtedly benefits associated with curiosity (scholarship, happiness, better health, and others). However, there is no proof that our curious nature demands that we find an answer to life's existential questions.

The scientific community generally agrees that curiosity is an *ingredient* in the development of well-being and meaning in life, but there is no evidence that *knowing* life's meaning is a core characteristic of being human.

Theological Purpose

Theologically, man's purpose is based heavily in scripture, divinity, and the supernatural. The term *man* has traditionally referred to humans in general, or humankind. Philosophically, it could be argued that our purpose is to fulfill our potential. But neither the theologian nor the philosopher *knows* their purpose in life—or if they even have one, other than that which they might define for themselves.

Theologians could speculate or even turn to religious texts for an answer to the question of why they are here on earth. Christians, for example, believe that life was not created by accident and that every person's life has purpose and meaning. That purpose, they argue, can be found in the Bible's Book of Mark, where Jesus says the foremost thing they should do in life is to: "... love the Lord your God with all your heart, and with all your soul, and with all your mind, and with all your strength.' The second is this, 'You shall love your neighbor as yourself.'"

Muslims also believe that Allah created everyone and everything for a reason, and that everyone has a purpose in life. In the Quran, 51:56, it states: "I created the jinn and humans for nothing else but that they may serve Me."

In Judaism, the answer is not as singular or clear. There are many answers to the question of life's purpose. However, most seem to embody the sentiment that the goal of Jewish life is *to embody Torah*, which Jewish people consider to be the living word of the living God.

While there is no broad agreement among all schools of Hindu philosophy, there are four generally agreed upon goals (purpose) of life to achieve in Hinduism:

- Kama. Obtaining enjoyment from life;

- Artha. Pursuing wealth and prosperity in one's life;

- Dharma. Acting virtuously and righteously, and repaying one's debt to the Gods and others; and

- Moksha. Seeking Enlightenment—the most important purpose in life—which may take *several lifetimes* to accomplish.

Buddhism teaches the knowledge and many lessons shared by The Buddha. The purpose in life, according to Buddhist teachings, can be found in his lessons. The most fundamental of The Buddha's teachings is that there are Four Aryan (or Noble) Truths: life is a struggle and full of suffering; the cause of suffering is our cravings and desires; the cessation of suffering is brought about by ceasing craving; and there is a path that leads from suffering. To find the meaning of life, they teach, we must release ourselves from the cycle of pain and suffering by becoming free of desire. The purpose of life, therefore, is to become kind, caring, and selfless, by helping others achieve freedom from suffering.

On the question of life's purpose, atheists, the nonreligious, the religiously unaffiliated, nonbelievers, and freethinkers are more likely to believe that life's meaning and purpose are **endogenous**: self-produced, originating internally. The purpose of life is whatever we determine it to be for ourselves.

The differences of perspectives about human beings' purpose in life raise two questions worth exploring:

1. Of the various sources of insight into life's purpose—Christianity, Islam, Judaism, Hinduism, Buddhism, the collective of nonbelievers and freethinkers—which is "right?"

2. Why do we need *any* purpose in life, not just preordained and definitive?

"The first step toward truth is doubt"

-DENIS DIDEROT-
French philosopher

The source of human beings' life purpose depends on one's life paradigm: a world view that provides an overall framework for helping us understand ourselves and the world around us, and helps us determine how to behave. Theists derive their life's purpose from their religion's scriptures. Secularists—if they do so at all—derive their life's purpose from what they determine is their path to leading a fulfilled life.

Theists face the interesting conundrum of fulfilling life's purpose based on the teachings of their particular religion without definitive knowledge of whether their religion's teachings are the teachings of the one "true" God. This supposes that there is *only* one God, which begs the question: Are there multiple Gods or is the Christian God, for instance, the same God worshiped in rival religions, such as Islam, Buddhism, Judaism, Confucianism, Yoruba Religion, and Daoism? If there are multiple Gods, whose scriptures differ, then there could be multiple conflicting, divinely-inspired purposes in life.

In his book "God is Not One: The Eight Rival Religions That Run the World," *New York Times* bestselling author and religion scholar Stephen Prothero argues that persistent attempts to portray all religions as different paths to the same God overlook the distinct problem that each tradition seeks to solve: the "same God" question. Whether or not all religions worship the same God is a question that theologians have explored for centuries without reaching a definitive answer. But what if Jesus Christ is God, as many Christians believe? If so, one can make the case that at least the Christian God and the Islamic God ("Allah") are likely not the same, because their teachings and texts are incompatible. In that case, both religions would argue that *their* version of the scripture is correct and *their* God is the one true God.

In this scenario, the various religions' beliefs of the truth and the singularity of their Gods are what are referred to in philosophy as *contraries*. Contraries (contrary statements) are a pair of propositions which cannot both be true, but can both be false. In other words, in a pair of contrary statements, the negation of one does not entail the other. The statements "My God is the one true God" by Christians and "My God is the one perfect God" by Muslims are contrary statements and, as such, they both cannot be true, but they *can* both be false. Logic dictates that if the seven aforementioned incompatible religions all claim the latter contrary statement that "My God is the one perfect God," then they cannot *all* be correct. Therefore, the former contrary statement is false. The later statement would also be false, since all religions cannot claim the one *true* God. In the case of these contraries, both statements could therefore be considered false.

Following this logic, either one religion's version of God is correct and the others are wrong, or all are wrong. This leaves room for other religions to make the case for why their rival religions' Gods are not the "true" God, because *their* God is the only true God. And, if they all believe that their Gods are the *one* true God—which they do—then, by extension of the preceding logic, *none* of their Gods can be the true God.

While I believe this contrary logic scenario is reasonable, to religious practitioners, it would not be considered rational. Assuming, however, that this contrary logic is reasonable to consider—as it is for nonbelievers and even some believers—then, by extension, *none* of the different life purposes and missions dictated by religious scriptures can be the **true purpose**. This means that no one—theists or freethinkers—can truly know life's definitive purpose, or if there actually *is* one.

Following this logic, either one religion's version of God is correct and the others are wrong, or all are wrong. And if they all believe that their Gods are the one true God—which they do—then, by extension of the preceding logic, none of their Gods can be the true God.

Assuming that this contrary logic is reasonable to consider then, by extension, none of the different life purposes and missions dictated by the religions' scriptures can be the true purpose, without an unequivocal global revelation. This means that no one—theists or freethinkers—can truly know life's definitive purpose, or if there actually is one.

CRISPR

When it comes to the existential question of human origin, we are all agnostic. None of us *know* how we got here or why. *Agnosticism* refers to knowledge, so when it comes to human origins or our purpose, no one can say with any degree of certainty that (1) they know that something or someone created us (a *creator*); (2) if there is a creator, they know that the creator created us for some specific reason and has given us a purpose; or (3) the creator in which they believe created humans for the exact same reason—*the same*—and with the same purpose in mind as the *other* various creators in which other people believe, even though the followers of the various creators believe different, conflicting doctrines.

So, since the various groups of people do not agree with or believe in the doctrines of the other peoples' creators, then, it can be argued that all human beings are, at our core, agnostic about (1) the existence of a creator, (2) whether the creator had a grand plan for human beings, or (3) what that plan could possibly be. Sure, people theologize, theorize, speculate, and guess at the purpose for which their version of a creator created human beings, but none of us *know*. The following scenario helps illustrate my point.

A new gene-editing tool called *clusters of regularly interspaced short palindromic repeats* (CRISPR"-Cas9) or "CRISPR" (pronounced "crisper"), which allows scientists to alter DNA sequences, holds promise for new disease treatments and the correction of genetic defects, as well as other life-altering benefits. Controversially, however, some scientists have used the scientific breakthrough in ways that have raised ethical questions.

In November 2018, Chinese researcher He Jianku modified a key gene in human embryos, producing genetically-edited babies. Since it is illegal to perform such experiments, Jiankui was found guilty and sentenced to three years in prison.

One of the major concerns about CRISPR-based clinical research is the potential for unrestrained scientists to use science to allow privileged parents to "customize" their children, creating a world of "perfect," privileged kids. While this sounds like the stuff of science-fiction movies, the potential exists.

Scenario #1: Imagine that you are a mad scientist with vast knowledge of genome editing and how to perform the CRISPR process. One day, you decided to go rogue and genetically modify human embryos to create what you believed would be the first humans in the world with immune systems so strong that they would defeat any invading pathogens, environmental assaults, infections, and viruses. With such immune systems, you believe that the genetically-modified human beings would live to be 150 years old.

To carry out your experiment, you somehow find egg donors and women willing to be gestational carriers or surrogates to carry the pregnancy and also provide eggs. Your plan is to create your own community in the most desolate, off-the-beaten-path, middle-of-nowhere place you can think of, like Glasgow, Montana, for example, where your CRISPR humans can live free from public and media scrutiny. Your sole purpose for engaging in the illegal experiment is to create a race of humans who can live to be 150 years old. And the CRISPR humans? Their purpose in life is *to live their lives in a manner that will enable them to reach the age of 150.* But there is a catch: although you have defined a specific reason for the humans' existence—why they were created, their purpose in life—*you never told them* what that purpose was.

By nature, human beings are a curious species. We are information-seekers. We hate not knowing things. Curiosity is such a fundamental aspect of our nature that we are practically blind to its pervasiveness and importance in our lives. Our curiosity motivates learning, which is necessary for good decision-making, and essential for our healthy development and survival. Not knowing things makes us uncomfortable. Consider this:

Suppose you and a friend rented a log cabin for the weekend in ... Glasgow, Montana; in the middle-of-nowhere. There are three doors in the cabin. One door leads to the bedroom, behind the second door is the bathroom, and the third door is locked. The question that will linger in your mind for the entire weekend is, "What's behind that locked door?" It will eat at you until you are able to open that door and see what's in there. And, if you are unable to open the door, your curiosity will almost certainly cause anxiety or even fear. But why? There are no noises, sounds, or odors emanating from behind the door. But, even still, the *not knowing* will drive you crazy.

Human beings need answers! What's behind that door (*perceptual curiosity;* an unpleasant state)? What's in that gift box I received (*epistemic curiosity;* a pleasurable state related to the expectation of a reward)? Where is Jimmy Hoffa buried? Who killed JFK? Is Bigfoot real? Is there a God? Where did we come from? What is my purpose in life?

As the CRISPR humans grow and start living their lives in their isolated Glasgow commune ("the commune"), inevitably they will start asking both existential and other questions, just like "normal" human beings: Where did human beings come from? What is my purpose in life? Why was I put here on planet earth? How the hell did we wind up living in *Glasgow, Montana*?

Although you, the mad scientist, created the CRISPR humans with a specific purpose for them to achieve (*live life to reach the age of 150*), you never told them the purpose. Without that specific knowledge from you—the person who defined their purpose—it would be impossible for them to guess their purpose. They might speculate that their purpose is to serve their "creator" (either you, the mad scientist who "created" them, or a deity), to build the commune into a loving, thriving society, or even to seek truth and wisdom. But it is unimaginable that they would *ever* guess that their purpose in life is to live to be 150 years old.

So, since they will never *know* their true purpose in life, any other *assumed* purpose which guides their life and behaviors would be misguided at best, and a waste of precious years of their lives, at worst; that is, unless they somehow miraculously guessed their preordained (by you), definitive purpose, or happen to define a meaningful purpose *for themselves.*

Not knowing whether humans, like the CRISPR humans, have any understood purpose for living, is the same as not having a purpose at all. If there is no definitive life purpose that is objectively known, the way that one decides to live his or her life will ultimately be decided *by that individual,* based on the reason(s) *they* determine for *themselves.*

Scenario #2. Now suppose that a second mad scientist (S2) created a community of new CRISPR humans for no other reason than the scientist wanted to see if they could successfully genetically modify human embryos and successfully bring them to term. S2 didn't want to create a human species that could live to be 150 years old, and the scientist had no expectations of the humans when they were born. The humans would not have a predetermined purpose in life.

In this scenario, the humans would have the same existential questions as the CRISPR humans in Scenario #1: Where did human beings come from? What is my purpose in life? Why was I put here on Earth? The only difference is that S2 did not assign a life purpose to the second group of humans.

This begs the question: Would the two groups of CRISPR humans live their lives differently? I believe that, in the absence of a preordained, objective, definitive life goal, purpose, or mission, both sets of CRISPR human beings would respond to their inner-most desires and aspirations to decide what brings them a sense of value, significance, joy and fulfillment, and establish those things as their life's purpose; all while taking into consideration the society to which they belong and the environment in which they live.

A COMPARISON OF TWO CRISPR POPULATIONS	
CRISPR Population #1	**CRISPR Population #2**
Given a preordained, specific life purpose: "Live life to reach the age of 150"	Not given a purpose
The purpose is not known	The purpose is not known
They will guess and then decide a life purpose or mission by and for themselves	They will decide a life purpose or mission by and for themselves
Their rational, intentional behavior will be directed at fulfilling their life's purpose	**Their rational, intentional behavior will be directed at fulfilling their life's purpose**

MEANING, RATIONALITY, FAITH, AND REASON

The need to find paradise elsewhere
is what keeps us from having it."

–TIBETAN SAYING–

THE MEANING *OF* LIFE VS. MEANING *IN* LIFE

Meaning *of* Life

Related to theories and questions about the purpose or meaning of life, philosophers often cite two different theories in an effort to answer the questions: God-centered theory and soul-centered theory.

God-centered theories state that the purpose and meaning of life are determined by supernatural Gods and passed down through scripture. Scriptures specifically (if not unambiguously) state that all life has meaning—even if the person does not know or understand it—and that the Gods have a plan for people's lives that involves some form of an articulated purpose. The reward for one's pursuit of fulfilling their purpose is eternal life; an afterlife.

In the Athenian philosopher Plato's The *Phaedo*—a philosophical dialogue involving Socrates—the concept of a *soul-centered theory* is presented. The theory proposes that human beings have an immortal soul that is separate from the physical body. Socrates believes that the purpose of life is to separate the soul from the body and to "dwell itself as far as it can both now and in the future." This suggests that, according to the soul-centered theory of the meaning of life, a person must *die* and become immortal to achieve meaningfulness. Put differently, Socrates proposes that the purpose of life is *death*.

Both God-centered and soul-centered theories about the purpose and meaning of life involve an afterlife and immortality—a condition, each proposes, for finding meaning in life. This implies that life on Earth has no meaning or purpose other than to get to the afterlife; to die.

Conversely, atheists' and freethinkers' position on immortality and an afterlife would seem to mirror that of Russian writer Leo Tolstoy, as he came to grips with his own mortality. In "A Confession," he wrote:

> Sooner or later there would come diseases and death ... to my dear ones and to me, and there would be nothing left but stench and worms. All my affairs, no matter what they might be, would sooner or later be forgotten, and I myself should not exist. So why should I worry about all these things?

While it is unlikely that non-believers and freethinkers would agree with the last sentence ("So why should I worry about all these things?"), implying that Tolstoy saw no reason for *living*, they would agree that when we die, in all likelihood, that's it. The end. This includes agnostics who might say that while they cannot know if there is an afterlife, they haven't been convinced of its existence or the existence of a God. Therefore, without incontrovertible proof, they believe that, when we die, that's it. The end. No afterlife.

God-Centered Theories	Soul-Centered Theories	Non-Believers
All life has meaning, a purpose, even if it is unknown. The reward for fulfilling the purpose is eternal life	Human beings have a soul. The purpose of life is to separate the soul from the body, or death.	It is not known if there is a definitive life's purpose, other than that which is self-determined. When you die, that's it.

Through whichever route one comes to grips with the meaning *of* life—something which both theists and non-believers all wonder about at some point in their lives—their revelation will inform their behaviors and thoughts to some degree. The pursuit of eternal life leads believers to behave in a manner consistent with their scripture's dictates. Those who are philosophically-inclined may seek deeper knowledge-of-self to gain insight into what can be done to preserve the soul after the physical body expires. And non-believers, who are uncertain about or don't believe in an afterlife, may decide that it is up to them to decide who and what they will be in life, and to behave accordingly. Ultimately, whether dogmatic or atheist, **human beings will decide** and pursue that which brings their life meaning and purpose. I say this because even if religious believers' behaviors are informed by their religion's scripture, the individual will have to *decide* (since they are free-willed) to do it before they will act on it.

"If I didn't define myself for myself, I would be crunched into other people's fantasies for me and eaten alive."

—Audre Lorde. The self-proclaimed *"black-lesbian feminist mother lover poet"*

Meaning *in* Life

Whereas the meaning *of* life relates to theism and, to a degree, existentialism—an exploration of human existence—meaning *in* life refers to **the pursuit and attainment of worthwhile goals**, leading to a sense of value, significance, and fulfillment. Within this definition is an assumption that one's actions adhere to some normative ethics or standards of rightness (rationality) and wrongness (irrationality) of actions in which one engages toward the pursuit of their goals.

A reasonable and practical framework for defining and establishing meaning *in* life has been developed by Paul Wang, Professor Emeritus of Trent University. His PURE strategy is a four-element approach that helps us comprehend the practicality of finding meaning in life without the necessity of or belief in immortality, nor the requirement that we die for it. According to Wang, the best way to define "meaning" is:

- Defining a practical, clearly-articulated *purpose* or life goal;

- *Understanding* who you are. Knowing yourself and having a clear concept of self-identity;

- Acting *responsibly* and doing what's "right" in light of your purpose and understanding; and

- Deriving *enjoyment* from your purpose, which boosts well-being. If enjoyment is low, reevaluate your goals.

Related to the human pursuit of life's meaning and purpose defined by one's paradigm regarding the meaning *of* life, to achieve meaning *in* life, one must intentionally **act in its pursuit**. So, whereas understanding the meaning *of* life is theoretical, achieving meaning *in* life is a practical pursuit.

THEORETICAL AND PRACTICAL RATIONALITY

Rationality is not a singular concept. Simplistically, rationality—the application of logic or reason—implies that an idea, thought, or opinion is well-considered and assessed before being formed or prior to an action being undertaken; this is one of the cognitive processes involved in rational thought. Though rationality can be *formal* or *substantive*, I will focus on *theoretical* and *practical* rationality because of its applicability to the discussion of thought leading to practice.

"Theoretical" means that the object of consideration is based on theories or supposition, as opposed to practical experience. It is concerned with the theory, concept, or philosophy of a subject area rather than its practical application. "Theoretical rationality" is displayed in governing one's logic- and reason-based beliefs or opinions, for example.

"Practical" means being concerned with actually doing or applying the object of consideration rather than its theory or approach. "Practical Rationality" is displayed in the logic and reason governing one's actions. Using logic and reason to understand the path to the Buddhist concept of enlightenment is an example of *theoretical* rationality; meditating and practicing yoga to get on the path of enlightenment is an example of *practical* rationality.

The comparison between theoretical and practical rationality is like the difference between a philosopher and a scientist. The purpose of philosophy is to seek knowledge and understanding. Philosopher William Halverson had an interesting take on the topic, writing: "Philosophy is man's quest for the unity of knowledge. Here is man, surrounded by the vastness of a universe in which he is only a tiny and perhaps insignificant part, and he wants to understand it."

Aristotle had a similar opinion to Halverson about a philosopher's purpose, but, like me, he compared it to science, in a sense: "A man who is puzzled and wonders thinks himself ignorant; therefore, since they philosophized in order to escape from ignorance, evidently they were pursuing science in order to know, and **not for any utilitarian end**."

With this statement, Aristotle suggests that philosophers seek knowledge and understanding to escape ignorance, and they conduct experiments for the sole purpose of *knowing*, not for *application*, as scientists do.

Therein lies the difference between the philosopher and the scientist: the scientist seeks to explain and predict for *utility* reasons; ways that knowledge can become practical and helpful, such as eradicating disease, for example. Knowing vs. learning and applying.

Meaning *of* Life	Meaning *in* Life
All life has meaning, a purpose, even if it is unknown. The reward for fulfilling the purpose is eternal life	Once human beings define life's meaning or purpose, they must intentionally act to pursue it
Theoretical Rationality (Knowing)	**Practical Rationality** (Learning and doing)

What roles do *faith* and *reason* play in our decision to pursue a particular life purpose or meaning; a pursuit which will inform the types of behavior that we engage in as we pursue purpose or mission?

FAITH, REASON, AND GOAL ATTAINABILITY

In her paper, *The Virtue of Practical Rationality*, philosopher Sigrún Svavarsdóttir argues that one of the failures that detracts from an actor's practical rationality is that the actor may fail to use his cognitive capacities in the context of his practical endeavors. This can be viewed differently, depending on one's paradigm. Limiting or failing to use one's cognitive capacity can negatively impact working memory and, therefore, one's ability to *reason*, since working memory and reasoning share cognitive capacity limits.

Reasoning, the central activity in intelligent thought, is a process used to draw inferences or conclusions from facts, agreed-upon data, observations, or self-evident proofs to establish a conclusion or achieve a *goal*. A **goal** is an intended outcome of an activity or endeavor in which one is engaged, such as the pursuit of life's purpose. Goals are necessary, because they establish what one is striving to accomplish and dictate behaviors in which they engage. For example, if a person's goal is to earn $1 million within a calendar year, that person will engage in activities and behaviors directly related to achieving that goal; earning $1 million. If another person's goal is to lose 20 pounds within six months, that person will engage in behaviors and activities that contribute to weight-loss. Goals dictate behaviors. Even unconscious goals—personal motivations of which one may be unaware—drive behavior and action.

In his 1943 paper *A Theory of Human Motivation* and his later book, "Motivation and Personality," psychologist Abraham Maslow proposed that all human behavior is motivated by need; specifically, a hierarchy of needs. He argued that physiological needs, security needs, social needs, esteem needs, and self-actualizing needs play a major role in motivating our behavior. He referred to it as a hierarchy – often depicted as a pyramid of needs – because our primary, basic physiological needs, such as the need for food, must be satisfied before we can move on to satisfy a higher-level need, such as the need for companionship. Maslow believed that needs create *instinctual behaviors* in people which motivate us to behave in a way that satisfies the needs; **goals.**

People pursue goals for specific reasons. Goal: I want to lose 20 pounds. Reason: so that I can lower my blood pressure and live a healthier life. Goal: I want to earn $1 million dollars. Reason: so that I can move my family into a better, safer home. A goal, such as "to fulfill my life's purpose," is a goal which one consciously defines for themself even if their definitions are rooted in their interpretation of a religious text.

In his 2002 best-selling book, "The Purpose Driven Life," popular Christian pastor Rick Warren explains that personal fulfillment, satisfaction, and meaning in life can only be achieved by accomplishing the five purposes (not *one*) that God placed you on Earth to perform: love God through worship; fellowship; become

Christ-like (discipleship); minister to others; and share God's message through evangelism. The reason why a believer would hope to fulfill these purposes is to ultimately walk with God in heaven. Warren then suggests that only *one* of these purposes can be done during one's time on Earth: ministering to others. This begs the question: Should all Christians become ministers as a means of achieving the desired end of personal fulfillment, satisfaction, and meaning in life?

"Ministering to others," as described in 1 Peter 4:10-11, instructs: "Each of you should use whatever gift you have received to serve others, as faithful stewards of God's grace in its various forms. If anyone speaks, they should do so as one who speaks the very words of God." The Church of Jesus Christ of Latter-Day Saints describes ministering as attending to the needs of others and "representing Jesus Christ and acting as His agents to watch over, lift, and strengthen those around us." Even though there are different definitions of *ministering*, many share the same idea: representing Jesus Christ.

According to Warren, ministering should be the main life purpose for those seeking meaning in life. Would doing so bring happiness here on Earth, even to those who do not have a "calling" to minister? Could Christians not have a meaningful, fulfilling life if they took a different path to finding fulfillment in life? Did Mahatma Gandhi not find meaning in his life or was he not fulfilled in his mission? Is he, therefore, in hell—if there is such a realm? Is that rational?

It cannot go unstated that Warren's and fellow religious practitioners' declarations of life's purpose derive credence from their *faith*.

"Faith" is a broad term. Generally, however, faith is synonymous with *trust*. A biblical definition of faith is "confidence in what we hope for and assurance about what we do not see." Philosophically, the term *faith* can take on various meanings, depending on the context and specific model of faith being characterized. Generally, when a layperson discusses their faith, or when faith is used in a religious context, the primary models of faith being referred to are:

- The "Belief" model: Belief that God exists;

- The "Hope" model: Hope that the God who saves exists;

- The "Doxastic Venture" model: Commitment beyond any evidence that God exists; and

- The "Special Knowledge" model: Faith as knowledge of specific truths, as revealed by God.

An underlying component of faith is an affective cognitive or psychological state—a state of feeling confident (belief) and trusting. Confidence, belief, and trust are *not* the cornerstones of proof, knowledge, or fact; these are the elements through which the **process of reasoning** draws inferences or conclusions.

Philosophers and theologians have long held an interest in the relationship between *faith* and *reason*, and how a rational person should treat claims by either source. Philosopher and theologian, Søren Kierkegaard, for instance, prioritizes *faith* over reason, even to the point at which faith's proposition becomes *irrational*. Philosopher and political theorist, John Locke, on the other hand, prioritized reasonableness to assess a doctrine's irrationality (i.e., conflict with itself or known facts), which he believed indicated that a doctrine was unsound.

Generally, there are four basic models of interaction between faith and reason: conflict (where objects say different things), incompatibility (objects cannot both be true), weak compatibility (some overlap of objects, but still distinct), and strong compatibility (objects have a connection or parity). The models' driving principles suggest that faith and reason are mostly incompatible. So, when it comes to defining specific goals by which to live, which is more *rational*: defining them based on faith or reason?

In one sense, **logic** is the application of reasoned thought as distinguished from irrational thought. Logical thinking is the process by which one consistently uses reasoning to reach a conclusion. It involves reason and sound judgment. Logical thinking—whether we are consciously aware when we are actively engaged in the activity or not—helps people to make responsible (moral, beneficial, and useful) decisions. We do this by incorporating the following tools into the decision-making process: our desired goals (outcomes); our unfulfilled needs; the activities or actions in which we can engage to satisfy the needs; and the expected effects or consequences of these actions if engaged in.

Because a life goal, mission, or purpose dictates behaviors, it should be clearly defined, realistic, and attainable during one's earthly lifetime. Otherwise, pursuing a vague, unattainable mission or purpose is mostly a waste of one's time, other than any residual value that can be derived from its pursuit.

One important question to ask about every goal that a person plans to pursue is this: **"How will I know that I have successfully accomplished the goal?"** If, after some designated period of time, such as the sunset of one's life, you will not know whether you have successfully accomplished a goal, mission, or purpose— or, you will not "know" until after you are dead—then I believe the pursuit of such a goal is irrational; unless one's purpose for pursuing the unattainable goal is simply learning and enjoying the journey. This is because the goals are unachievable. It would be like traveling to find the lost Tibetan paradise *Shangri-la* (Shambala), even though the fabled utopia likely does not exist and would be, therefore, unreachable.

Shambala is, supposedly, located in the remotest part of Tibet in the Himalayas; actually, no one *knows* where it is located or if it now or has ever existed. The Dalai Lama says of Shambala:

"Although it is said to exist, people cannot see it, or communicate with it in an ordinary way. Some people say it is located in another world, others that it is an ideal land, a place of the imagination. Some say it was a real place, which cannot now be found. Some believe there are openings into that world which may be accessed from this."

Filmmaker Laurence Brahm produced a documentary titled "Searching for Shangri-La," chronicling a 2002 expedition seeking to answer one question: Where is Shangri-la? Ultimately, the expedition team determined that Shangri-la could not be found. As one Buddhist monk interviewed in the film explained, "To find the real Shangri-la, I think this world is heaven; our heaven. Is not far away."

If one's life purpose was to find Shangri-la in the hopes of experiencing eternal bliss, only to discover—after a lifetime spent pursuing the goal—that it is unattainable, would the explorer consider it to have been a worthwhile endeavor? Could the pursuit have even been unhealthy?

In their 2017 study, "Let It Go: Depression Facilitates Disengagement from Unattainable Goals," researchers Katharina Koppe and Klaus Rothermund found that people may develop clinical depression as a result of seriously pursuing an unattainable goal (like searching for Shangri-la) because, regardless of how much time and effort they put into the pursuit, their efforts will always be out of reach; pointless. They suggest that the experience can lead to feelings of hopelessness and helplessness. To reiterate, there *could* be value in the goal-pursuit itself, however.

Others, like Carol Dweck, bestselling author of "Mindset: The New Psychology of Success," for instance, might say that rebounding from failure is healthy, because it fosters a "growth mindset." Yet, others, like psychologist Jeffrey Bernstein, author of the book, "10 Days to a Less Defiant Child," argues that aspiring to achieve goals beyond our current station is life is healthy. However. aspiring to goals that are ridiculous and *unachievable* can lead to misery.

Although "to learn and live my life's purpose" can be a noble pursuit, the question remains: is it attainable or *reasonable*, if one's life purpose is incomprehensible, unknown, or not knowable? If it is incomprehensible at best, then what actions or behaviors would one exhibit in the direct pursuit of achieving the incomprehensible, unknown, or unknowable? For example, if one's life purpose or mission is to find Shangri-La, how would the person know what to do to get to the unreachable place? If the answer is unknown or unknowable, the actions or behaviors needed to get there are unknowable. Therefore, is it reasonable or rational to hold a mission like "finding Shangri-La" as one's life purpose?

Meaning, rationality, faith, and reason
not only lead people formulate an opinion
of life's meaning and purpose, but also
to decide how best to actually achieve
it; the actions or behaviors that will lead
to the achievement of the goal, mission,
purpose, or desired outcome.

Meaning *of* Life	Meaning *in* Life
All life has meaning, a purpose, even if it is unknown. The reward for fulfilling the purpose is eternal life	Once human beings define life's meaning or purpose, they must intentionally act to pursue it
Theoretical Rationality (Knowing)	**Practical Rationality** (Learning and doing)
Faith (Confidence, belief, and trust)	**Reason** (Proof, knowledge, fact)

A comparison of the meaning *of* life versus the meaning *in* life illustrates that whether or not people are preordained with a life meaning or purpose, human curiosity will lead them to take the knowledge (theoretical rationality and faith) gained from all sources and determine what they believe is the practical application of that knowledge (practical rationality and reason). The practical application of pursuing meaning in life will be based in learning, knowledge, doing, proof, and fact, which are all practical and reasonable.

THREE CRISPR COMMUNITIES

Let's revisit the scenario of the CRISPR mad scientist who created a community of people with the potential of living for 150 years. The life purpose he defined for the genetically-modified people was "*to live their lives in a manner that will enable them to reach the age of 150.*" I will refer to this CRISPR community as the "150 Community" (or the "150s").

The second mad scientist, "S2," also created a CRISPR community, but hers was different. This scientist only wanted to see if she could clone humans that would be brought to term as living people; that's it. She defined no life purpose for her community, who also lived in Glasgow. I will refer to this community as the "Clones."

Now suppose that a third, egomaniacal, mad scientist suffering from the narcissistic personality disorder of a "god complex"—believing he is a god—decided to conduct an experiment similar to the other scientists, and create a CRISPR community of people for no other reason than to reinforce his belief that he is a god. This community also lives in Glasgow, Montana. The egomaniacal mad scientist defined his CRISPR humans' life purpose as: "Convince *the rest of the Glasgow community that they should worship me.*" However, the narcissist only told one convincer about their purpose, and left it up to that person to spread the word. I will refer to this community as the "Convincer Community" (or the "Convincers").

The Convincers do not know why the mad scientist wants everyone to worship him. However, most of them believe that, by worshiping him and convincing the other non-Convincer Glasgow residents to do the same, the Convincers will somehow find happiness in the process.

The 150s who, in this scenario know their life's purpose, believe that the way to live for 150 years is to eat a plant-based, whole food, unprocessed, vegan diet.

The Convincers catch wind of their own purpose (*"Convince the rest of the Glasgow community that they should worship me."*) through the grapevine, and most of them believe it to be true. So, they engage in the daily practice of corner-preaching and other marketing to achieve their purpose. The Clones, who possessed no definitive life purpose, were left to create one for themselves, based on what they believe will bring them fulfillment.

Four questions to consider

1. What will happen over time as the three communities begin to interact with and live among each other? They will naturally inform the others about their community's life purpose. Which purpose, if any, do you believe will ultimately win the day and become the most appealing and desirable to all within the community?

2. At some point, will the Convincers begin to question whether their purpose—that they learned about through the grapevine—brings them more happiness and life satisfaction than spending their lives doing something different? Will they question whether their purpose is even true and if there is more to life than promoting a narcissistic mad scientist? Will their doubt lead them to change their life's purpose to something more tangible and aligned with their interests or at which they have natural talent or the capacity to excel?

3. Will the 150s who have become skinny, anemic, iron-deficient, and brittle-boned begin to question whether the addition of fish or meat into their diet will make them healthier and more energetic? Though they are CRISPR humans, they are still *human*, and possess **vanity, uncertainties, temptations, curiosities,** and **fallibilities** like any other human being. Will the temptation of Chick-fil-A nuggets or a Big Mac lead them to begin sampling non-vegan foods? Will they enjoy the non-vegan foods and modify their prescribed purpose (and its associated behaviors) to one that makes them feel happier and more fulfilled?

4. How will the Clones, who have no predetermined life purpose, determine *their* individual life purposes?

Ultimately, I believe that everyone in the Glasgow community will define, redefine, reshape, or modify a life purpose that **they decide for themselves**. They are human. They will define a mission or purpose that will give their lives greater meaning, happiness, and fulfillment, and is more closely aligned to what they are intrinsically predisposed to value. This, I believe, is not only a logical expectation, but also a rational one.

Reason-Based Practical Rationality: Advice to Our Younger Selves

Although one may define their life's mission or purpose based either in the faith or reason domain, ultimately, the greater certainty of practically-rational outcomes will supersede a theoretically-rational belief (such as admission into an afterlife). This will lead people to modify their life's purpose to that which is more evidentially tenable. This is a natural inclination based on the times in which we live, our life experiences, and our *humanness.* Human beings need to see or feel an impact from our goal-directed actions to continue down the specific path of accomplishing that goal. Whether the goal is divinely-inspired or personally-defined, people will change course to pursue one which achieves tangible results.

Proverbs 28:19 from The Bible states that "Those who work their land will have abundant food." In 2015, a Wisconsin farmer named Craig Myhre was trying to make a living off a 600-acre farm that has been in his family since 1952. Despite working 16-hour days to support his family of five children, Myhre could not make ends meet solely from the farm, "I struggle to pay myself sometimes," he said. So, he added another job as a mail carrier to help sustain his family.

According to the U.S. Department of Agriculture, on average, 82% of U.S. farm household income comes from off-farm work, such as being a mail carrier, for example. If Myhre's life purpose was to "work their land" and have "abundant food," enough that would enable his family to live comfortable lives off the farm, when he realized that fulfilling that purpose solely from the land was untenable, he modified his goal to something more practical.

Scarcity drives human thought away from strategic, long-term goals, and toward more urgent needs of the moment. If, for example, you had $300 to spend on groceries for a week's worth of meals for your five-person family, your shopping list would look radically different than if money was scarce and you had only $20 to spend on groceries. When your money is abundant (e.g., $300 for one week's groceries), you might buy some steaks and splurge on a couple bottles of wine, and maybe even some crème brûlée for dessert. And whatever money is left over, you'd just put away in junior's college fund. When money is scarce (e.g., $20 for the week), you will be forced to focus on the basics to stretch that $20. **Practical**. No steak. No wine. No college fund savings. No thinking about food for *next* week.

The same concept applies with the scarcity of time. When people who have more life behind them than ahead start thinking about their mortality, their actions and behaviors will likely shift from pursuing long-term or aspirational goals, to more tactical things that will bring them happiness and satisfaction in the remainder of *this* lifetime. So, while faith remains of utmost importance for many people facing their mortality, their life's behaviors become focused on things that bring them earthly-fulfillment in the present, rather than on the pursuit of uncertainty about what will happen when we die.

In 2020, AARP, a nonprofit interest group focused on issues affecting those over the age of 50, established an affiliation with the Colorado-based charity Wish of a Lifetime (WOL) that grants the wishes of seniors age 65 and older. WOL aims to "help renew a **sense of purpose** and belonging in the older adults this program serves," said AARP board chair Annette Franqui.

Franqui's description prompts the question: What becomes of the "sense of purpose" for people when life is short and time is precious? Do they stick with their original life's mission or purpose pursued since childhood or young adulthood, or do they modify it based on the times or their stage or station in life?

One way to answer the question is empirically, by asking people in their sunset years what advice they would give to young people or their younger selves, who, unlike themselves, have a long life ahead of them. In their report entitled "If I knew then what I know now: Advice to my younger self," psychologists Robin Kowalski and Annie McCord presented these conclusions in *The Journal of Social Psychology*. The study shows that advice from people who are 30 years or older is consistent with the findings of studies showing people's biggest life regrets. Both sets of findings focus on **practical behaviors** that yield tangible, gratifying outcomes. The respondents' recommendations centered around five general categories:

Relationships	Direction and goals
Education	Saving money
Self-worth ("Follow your own path" and "Be yourself")	

The advice-giving respondents stated that following the advice would bring them closer to their ideal self than the self they believed they were expected or supposed to be. They also believed that following their advice would lead to more *positive perceptions of the self*.

I was not surprised that, when faced with a scarcity of time or having experienced real life with all of its ups and downs, the respondents' recommendations were practical and reasonable, based on knowledge—the result of their life-experience. However, it was somewhat surprising that there was very little mention of spirituality and faith.

An adage I share with others as they pursue their personal or work-related mission, goal, or purpose is: Any activity that is not in direct support of accomplishing a goal or achieving an objective is wasted effort.

No one expends every ounce of their energy pursuing a goal or purpose. We are not machines. The sentiment of the adage is what's important. The best way to achieve success—defined as accomplishing a predefined goal or achieving an objective—is to ensure that one allocates time toward completing specific activities that, when completed, will get a person one step closer to their desired outcome. For example, if I defined my life's purpose as *achieving ultimate value or significance by lifting and keeping an underserved, impoverished neighborhood out of poverty*, and I decided that to do so I would have to earn $1 million, I would focus my efforts on earning $1 million. In this example, my ultimate purpose— to achieve value and significance—drove my behavior. And even if, in my pursuit of significance, I made some irrational decisions, I would have done so in its pursuit.

In the CRISPR community scenario, after the people have defined, redefined, reshaped, or modified their life's purpose, their pursuit of that purpose will drive their actions and behaviors, both rational and irrational.

PURPOSE-DRIVEN BEHAVIOR

Any activity in which we engage that is not in direct support of accomplishing a goal or achieving an objective is wasted effort."

-EDWARDS-

braham Maslow famously proposed that all human behavior is motivated by need. While this concept is widely accepted as valid, on a more granular, practical level, I believe there needs to be a planning and actionable element in such a model. This is because, in the pursuit of accomplishing a goal or achieving a mission or purpose, one's behavior will be directed toward those ends, if accomplishing the goal, mission, or purpose is deemed important to the person who defines it. The activities or behaviors one exhibits in this goal, mission, or purposeful pursuit are **purpose-driven behavior**. It is the behavior that is necessary to achieve a goal, mission, purpose or other desired outcome.

Purpose-driven behavior is consistent with "habitual behavior," which is behavior that is displayed automatically in the presence of a goal. Within habitual behavior, as with purpose-driven behavior, there is a direct goal–action link (see the illustration on a following page). However, unlike with purpose-driven behavior, habitual behavior is *not* preceded by consciously developed intentions. This is due to the routine or automatic nature of habitual behavior.

In their paper "Habitual Behavior Is Goal-Driven," researchers Kruglanski and Szumowska presented findings, published in *Perspectives on Psychological Science*, which make the case that "habitual behavior is sensitive to changes in goal properties (reward contingencies), namely goal value and its expectancy of attainment." The implications of their findings for one's goal, mission, and purpose are that, depending on one's expectation of actually *achieving* a goal, mission, or purpose, one's behavior will change accordingly.

Imagine, for example, that a person establishes a life goal of "transforming into the likeness of Christ" by working within this world to restore it to the way God created it to be. Now suppose that, over time, the person comes to believe that such a goal is unattainable, and changes their goal to something they believe they can realistically achieve. By doing so, they will find satisfaction and fulfillment. In such cases, the *realistically-attainable* goal that the person redefines for themself will be practical and based on things from which the person derives self-worth and value. If the redefined goal, mission, or purpose is so lofty that, although the person believes it to be attainable, the person has not received any positive feedback or results from their purpose-driven efforts, the person will likely ratchet down their goal to something that does provide them with a payoff.

To reiterate, if people do not see an impact from their efforts, they will likely change their goal (i.e., course-correct) to something that provides positive, motivating feedback from the effort they expend in its pursuit.

Needs inform purpose, purpose dictates process, and process drives actions and behaviors. Actions and behavior complete a process. A completed process fulfills a purpose, and a fulfilled purpose satisfies the need. However, if one's actions do not complete a process, a person will change their actions. If one's actions *do* complete a process, but the process does not fulfill a purpose, the person will define a new process. And, if one's actions, process, and purpose are all successful, but the need is not satisfied, the person will repeat the process, beginning with their actions, behaviors, and process—assuming their purpose is valuable to their notion of self. This logic is demonstrated through the example of hunger.

Over time, if the person comes to believe that a goal is unattainable, they will change their goal to something they believe they can realistically attain; and by doing so, they will achieve satisfaction and fulfillment. In such cases, the *realistically-attainable* goal that the person redefines for themself will be practical and based on those things from which the person derives self-worth and value. And if the redefined goal, mission, or purpose is so lofty that, although the person believes it to be attainable, the person has not received any positive feedback or results from their purpose-driven efforts, the person will likely ratchet down their goal to something that provides them with a payoff from their work.

Maslow states that our basic physiological need of hunger will motivate us to behave in a manner that satisfies hunger, by eating and drinking. I propose that a planning aspect such as "what" and "how," including cause-and-effect logic, is needed. This gives the person an ability to satisfy their hunger as efficiently and effectively as possible by forcing them to apply human logic to the endeavor.

- **Intrinsic Need:** Hunger

- **Purpose**: What are you trying to accomplish? *Answer:* Satisfy my hunger.

- **Process:**

  - How will you satisfy your hunger? **A:** by eating and drinking.

  - What is the cause-and-effect (or "If-Then") logic to secure your food and drink? **A:** If I go fishing and catch some fish and then cook it, I will be able to eat.

- **Action or Behavior**: Catch a fish, cook it, and eat it. However, if I cannot catch a fish, I will change my behavior and process by stealing some food from the store (an irrational behavior), because I have no money and I am hungry.

In this simple example, the person's hunger need drove them to define a purpose to satisfy their hunger. They then identified what was needed to satisfy the hunger (food and drink), and applied logic to determine necessary actions or behaviors to get the food and drink (catch a fish or steal the food and cook it). This purpose-driven behavior is illustrated below.

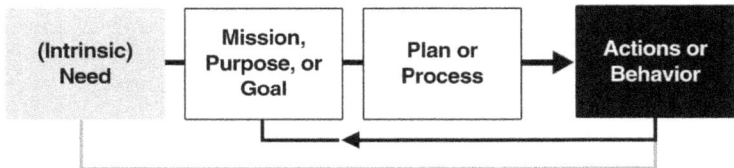

Although this example is simplistic, it nonetheless represents the process that people go through when they identify an intrinsic need and determine a mission, purpose, or goal, and plan how best to achieve it. If a pursuit is worth achieving, it is worth planning for. If high school junior Kate's foreseeable mission is to play soccer in college, she would go through the same process—mentally or documented—to give herself the best chance of achieving the desired outcome:

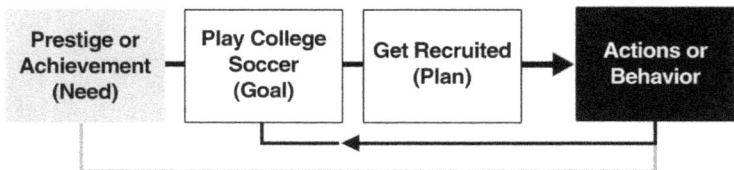

As we mature and gain life experiences, we get better at conceptualizing the actions that must be performed in pursuit of a mission or purpose, or to accomplish a goal. Over time and with life experience, once we have decided on what we hope to become, possess, or achieve, our behaviors toward those ends become—in many cases—instinctual.

For example, if someone wants to improve their self-confidence (the need) and decides to become healthy (purpose or goal) and lose weight (the process), the person will know several things to do, actions to take, or behaviors in which to engage to reach that end. When they do, they will perform the actions instinctively, without needing a detailed plan—although a documented plan can be of great value. If a person wanted to feel empowered (need) and summit Mount Everest (purpose or goal), the person would determine the time commitment, preparation, cost, training, and other actions necessary (plan or process) to best position themselves to succeed at that incredible challenge. Then, the person will perform the process (actions or behaviors). If another person wanted to become more "likeable"— however the person defines it—the person will begin thinking of things they can do toward that end, instinctively, even if their instinctual or even documented and planned actions or behaviors are considered irrational.

That's one of the interesting aspects of one's pursuit of a mission, purpose, or goal: oftentimes, that pursuit may be so difficult to achieve rationally that people will act irrationally if they believe attaining the desired out-come is important to their **notion of self**. Such behav-ior could create an internal conflict: "Behaving badly might decrease my sense of self, which I am trying to improve." This is an example of how, in defending or enhancing one's sense of self, rational people can be-have irrationally, which is the very premise of this book.

PART TWO

SELF AND SIGNIFICANCE

SELF-CONCEPT AND WORTHINESS

THE CONCEPT OF "SELF" AND WORTHINESS

*H*uman beings are inherently social beings. We rely on others for care, comfort, safety, and security. As Maslow proposed in "A Theory of Human Motivation," human beings have an inherent need for love and social belonging, which motivates us to seek companionship and relationships with others. It is through our relationships and interactions with others that humans develop a mental conception of *self*: our beliefs about our own worthiness for care and lovability.

The concept of self—*Self-Concept*—provides context and insight into how people determine roles in social structures and form social identities. A person's social identity provides a person with a sense of who they are based on the group(s) or community(ies) of which they are a part. Social identity groups are normally defined by the common characteristics of members of the group, such as race, ethnicity, gender, religious beliefs, sexual orientation, sports, and others. This aligns with Maslow's theory of social belonging in the sense that people have an intrinsic need for social group acceptance that satisfies our need for love, belonging, connection, friendship, and trust.

When we develop a social identity, we can then categorize and compare ourselves to others within our social structure or group, helping us refine an identity. Through our identity, the *self* occupies a role within the group, a role that incorporates meaning and expectations, forming standards that guide behavior. When people develop a social identity, it is common for people within a social structure to go through a cognitive process called *depersonalization*, in which we see the self as an embodiment of in-group norms, rather than as a unique individual. The group's standards and behaviors become more influential in the definition of self than a person's own individual standards. When this happens, a person's notion of self-worthiness can be influenced externally, by their group standing.

Our *intrinsic* notion of self is correlated with self-worthiness or *self-worth*, an internal feeling of being good enough and worthy of the love of others and social belonging. Self-worth is a function of our psychological need for love, validation. This differs from self-esteem, which often relies on *extrinsic* factors, such as achievements, material possessions, and praise from others to define our worth. The relationship between self-worth and self-esteem lies in the notion that a person's group identity and its norms can guide an individual's behavior, just as extrinsic factors. With that as a premise, a person's feelings of worthiness can influence their perception of self, the need to belong, and ultimately, their self-esteem and happiness.

Self-Esteem

Self-esteem research has been conducted for decades. Yet, there is no consensus on a definition for this construct. For this reason, I will refer to self-esteem as an overall reflection of an individual's self-worth; their beliefs about themselves, their capacity to feel worthy of love, belonging, and happiness, and their ability to successfully navigate life's challenges.

When the value we ascribe to ourselves hinges on external factors, our own value can be unpredictable, often subjective, and inconsistent, leading to struggles with feelings of worth. It can leave one feeling empty. Our intrinsic notion of self is highly correlated with self-esteem: people with a positive intrinsic notion of self (secure individuals) have higher self-esteem than those with a negative intrinsic notion of self (anxious, ambivalent, or overly needy individuals).

Secure individuals—those who inherently believe they are wonderful—have high self-esteem and are less likely to base their self-esteem on external domains. Instead, they base self-esteem on how they feel about themselves based on the mental model of their intrinsic self and their self-knowledge of their worthiness for love and social belonging. Consider 1960s boxing upstart Cassius Clay, later known as Muhammad Ali, who would become the "greatest" heavyweight boxing champion of all time.

In 1964, contender Cassius Clay, prior to joining the Nation of Islam or "Black Muslim" religious group and changing his name to Muhammad Ali, was scheduled to face the fearsome heavyweight champion Charles "Sonny" Liston. The hard-punching Liston was considered unbeatable, having easily knocked out 27 fighters in his 35 wins prior to the Clay fight. On the night of the fight, February 25th, Liston was a prohibitive 7-to-1 betting favorite to beat the braggadocious Clay. Of the 46 sportswriters seated at ringside that night, 43 picked Liston to win by knockout. Both boxing fans and casual observers alike—especially the masses who despised the loud, brash Clay—thought this would be the night he got his comeuppance. Unfortunately for them, Sonny Liston retired on his stool at the end of the seventh round; Clay had predicted before the match that he would stop Liston in the eighth. He had "shook up the world," defeating Sonny Liston by technical knockout.

In the 1960s, many Americans were turned-off by Cassius Clay, even before his conversion to The Nation of Islam and proclaiming that white men were "white devils." He was a boorish braggart in their opinion: as early as his first professional fight, he repeated the refrain that he was "... young. I'm handsome. I'm fast. I can't *possibly* be beat." He shamed 12 of his first 19 opponents by correctly predicting the exact round in which he would knock them out. He was arrogant and unapologetic, the exact opposite of the docile, well-behaved—but loved—former champion Floyd Patterson. This was an era when white Americans preferred influential black public figures to be humble and compliant. Clay was the opposite, and he let everyone know that he did not care what they thought of him. "It's hard to be humble when you're as great as I am," he would say.

Prior to the Liston fight, Clay's advisors, trainers, and investors implored him to tone down the rhetoric and be humbler and more publicly deferential to Liston. They believed Clay's dismissive behavior toward Liston ("[Sonny Liston] is too ugly to be the world champ. The world champ should be pretty, like me!") would awaken and anger "the big ugly bear." Plus, they said, humility would help with his public appeal, wider acceptance, and marketability. But Clay ignored their advice. His mental model of his intrinsic self was positive and *strong*. He understood his self-worth. He knew who he was as a man, and no one's opinion of him, no one's distaste for his arrogance, no one's desire for him to be meek and less threatening, and no one's demands that he "shut up!" could affect the greatness that he knew he possessed. No external influences could impact his self-worth or self-esteem.

Self-Worth and Self-Esteem

Maslow proposed that approval from others (and thus, their opinions of us) gives us a higher sense of self-worth and satisfies our need for respect from others. For many people, others' approval plays a role in how they value themselves, and matters in the determination of their self-worth. To Maslow, this satisfies their *esteem* need.

If strong, positive, self-knowing individuals like Cassius Clay exist at one end of the self-esteem/self-worth spectrum, at the opposite end of the spectrum are often teenagers and young adults whose intrinsic self-worth and general feelings about themselves are more easily influenced by *external factors* than is the case with a more secure individual like Cassius Clay, for instance.

Personality and Social Psychology Bulletin published a 2014 study of teenagers and young adults in 19 countries. The study revealed that, regardless of one's personal values, teens and young adults generally base their self-esteem on cultural values; self-esteem is externally influenced rather than intrinsically defined, meaning that the way teens and young adults feel about themselves is based on measuring up to the values and standards of people with whom they interact in their cultural environments. Therefore, since how they feel about themselves—good or bad—is externally influenced, those external, societal influences affect their self-esteem, which impacts their self-worth, and ultimately, influences their intrinsic notion of self.

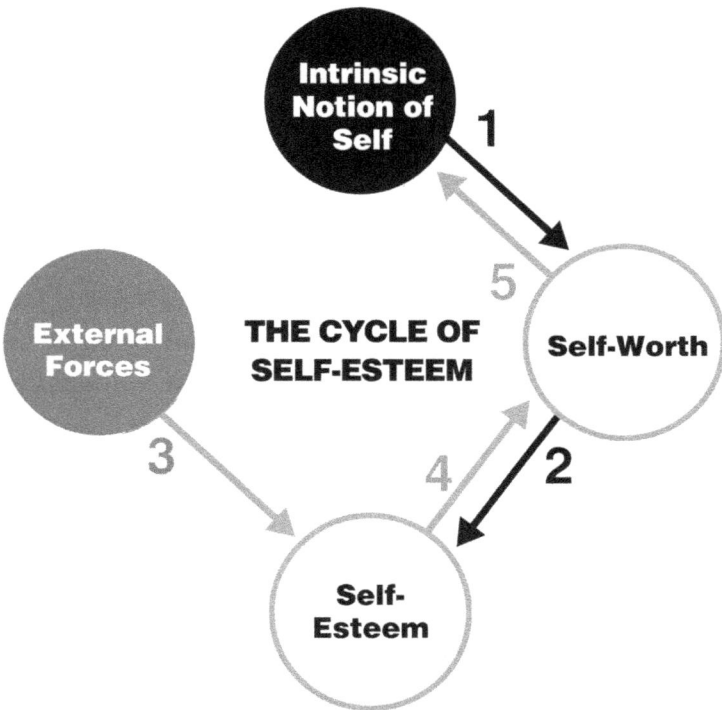

Intrinsic Notion of Self

1

5

External Forces

THE CYCLE OF SELF-ESTEEM

Self-Worth

3

4

2

Self-Esteem

In situations in which one's self-worth depends on meeting some standard of societally-defined constructs—called *domains*—teens and young adults will decide on which domains they will stake their self-worth. For example, a student's self-esteem may depend on meeting some social media or other societally-defined standard of being "attractive," smart, or god-fearing. For another student, their self-esteem or worth could be contingent upon being athletically-elite or confident. Such *contingencies of self-worth* become goals that people feel they must accomplish to have high self-esteem. When people are dependent on cultural influences or conditions defined by other people to achieve satisfaction and feel good about themselves, externally-defined domains may be associated with lower-levels of psychological well-being in young people than it is with people who base their satisfaction on intrinsic aspects of self.

Positive self-esteem is related to better health, lower levels of depression, and a happier, more fulfilling life. However, if the way a person feels about themselves leads to feelings of low self-worth and low self-esteem, feelings can not only lead to a lower quality of life, but, unchecked, can lead to mental health issues, such as anxiety and depression. It can also lead to poor decision-making. The good news for young adults is that self-esteem rises steadily as people age.

A paper published by the American Psychological Association titled, "Self-esteem Declines Sharply among Older Adults while Middle-Aged Are Most

Confident," reported that self-esteem was lowest among young adults, and that it "increased throughout adulthood, peaking at age 60, before it started to decline." Additional research published by Crocker, Cooper, and Bouvrette in the *Journal of Personality and Social Psychology* identified seven bases of self-esteem on which college students (i.e., teens and young adults) derive self-worth:

- Academics
- Appearance
- Approval from others
- Competition
- Family support
- God's love
- Virtue

Positive events, responses, or successes in these domains influence and boost self-esteem, mood, and self-evaluative thoughts, which positively impact how they feel about themselves and their self-worth. Negative responses in these domains can have the opposite effect, and negatively impact one's intrinsic model of self-worth. For example, suppose that Jim's college fraternity brother gave him negative feedback that, "Although it's true that you are the top student in this college by a mile and will be graduating Summa Cum Laude, *saying* that you're the smartest student in the school is off-putting to other students, which is hurting your reputation. So, you should not say that anymore." Jim, who lacks assurance about his intrinsic self, would allow such feedback to affect his self-esteem to the point where he not only stops making the proclamation, but also feels less about himself as a person for potentially hurting other students' feelings, *even though he is factually the smartest person at the college.*

In this example, Jim's low-confidence model of his intrinsic self and, therefore, his own self-worth allows his worth to be, at least in part, defined by external factors, such as *the approval of others.* The disapproval of others affects his self-esteem which, in turn, negatively impacts his self-assurance, downwardly affecting his definition of self. This further erodes Jim's self-assurance and, ultimately, his self-worth.

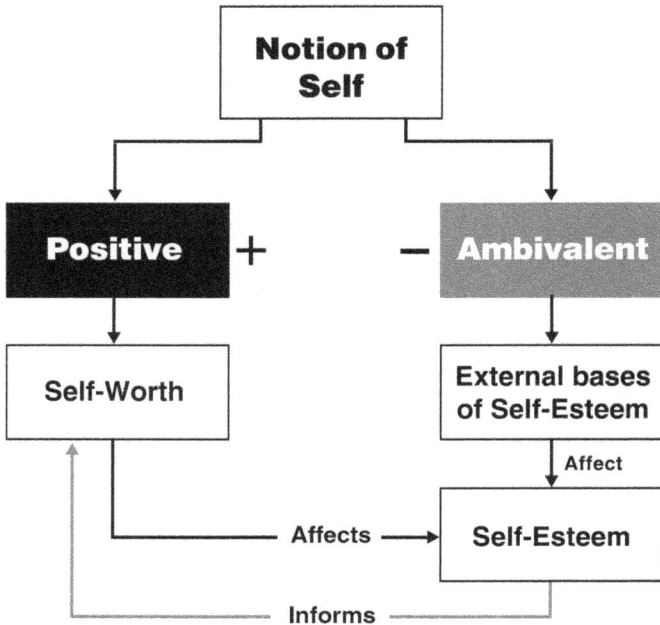

On the other hand, when braggadocious behavior could lose the approval of others, instead of cowering to the dictates of the disapprovers, self-assured individuals, like Cassius Clay/Muhammad Ali, might double down: "I'm not the greatest, I'm the *double* greatest. Not only do I knock 'em out, I pick the round."

Positive mental images of oneself translate into feelings of self-satisfaction in the domain in which the person considers oneself. For example, if the person has a notion of self as being one of the foremost thinkers in the field of Biophysics, the person will feel at peace and satisfied with their level of intelligence and degree of scientific knowledge. This self-assuredness and confidence contribute to the person's sense of worth. They have merit, are useful to society, and are therefore valued. This self-assuredness contributes to one's positive self-esteem. Contrarily, an ambivalent notion of self can open the door to one's self being informed by external influences on self-esteem, such as a teen or young adult believing that, to be attractive and desirable, one must look like the stereotypical social media model. If the person comes to believe that s/he is not social media model-like in appearance, feelings of inadequacy in this domain could lower the person's self-esteem and eventually their self-worth.

Secure individuals with a strong mental model of their intrinsic self and their worthiness are less likely to base their self-esteem on external domains than they are to base it on their own determinants of self. These people are referred to as *self-validating*. To quote self-described "Black, lesbian, mother, warrior, poet" Audre Lorde, in a 1982 speech at Harvard University: "That is how I learned that if I didn't define myself for myself, I would be crunched into other people's fantasies for me and eaten alive." Self-assured individuals, like Lorde and Ali, derive their "definitions of themselves" *by* themselves. But such self-assured individuals are in the minority.

The Pervasiveness of Low Self-Esteem

Measuring a person's self-esteem is challenging, especially when researchers utilize *self-reported* measures of self-esteem. Such assessment methods are often arbitrary. Therefore, it is difficult—if at all possible—to definitively determine whether study participants absolutely had low or high self-esteem, or if their measure of self-esteem was based on specific factors associated with self-esteem (e.g., weight status) which places them into the category of fundamentally having low self-esteem.

Estimates of the total number of Americans with low self-esteem vary widely: A 2010 study published in the journal *Academic Pediatrics* suggests that, on average, across race and gender, 21% of respondents experience low self-esteem. The *Dove Global Beauty and Confidence Report* found that 50% of the women surveyed had low self-esteem and 70% of girls aged 8 to 17 have some degree of low self-esteem. Less reliably, though no less intriguing, self-esteem author Dr. Joseph S. Rubino estimates that 85% of the world's population are *affected by* low self-esteem. Though different research reveals different self-esteem findings based on the metrics used and the desired research outcome, a consistent claim across all research is that most Americans' self-worth is significantly affected by their self-esteem. There does, however, exist dependable research which reveals useful insights into the pervasiveness of some impactful degree of low self-esteem in individuals.

The research suggests that most Americans have an ambivalent notion of self, where their self-worth is informed by and reflects their self-esteem. The self-esteem of people with an ambivalent notion of self is influenced and formed by external factors that affect the way they think about themselves, the **value they ascribe to themselves**, their general opinion of themselves, and their overall feeling of personal worthiness.

Worth. Usefulness/Purpose. Value.

If, as I define it, self-esteem is an overall reflection of and a contributor to an individual's self-worth, then it is reasonable to believe that people with the capacity to intrinsically drive their self-esteem are more likely to see themselves as worthy, valued members of society compared with those individuals whose self-esteem is externally driven. Self-driven people are more fulfilled than those who derive self-esteem from extrinsic sources. Consider Crocker, Cooper, and Bouvrette's seven bases of self-esteem from which college students derive self-worth: academics, appearance, approval from others, competition, family support, god's love, and virtue. Other people's opinions about how these bases apply to the students can impact the students' self-esteem, contributing to their intrinsic definition of their worth, their *value*.

By definition, **"value"** is the *relative* worth, utility, or importance of something. The word "relative" is important because it reminds us that, at the individual level, value is often defined through the eyes of the beholder or the self: what is considered valuable by one person may not be considered valuable by another. On a societal or group level, however, the concept of that which is valuable is generally agreed upon. Universally, food is highly valued and necessary. In developed economies, such as the Group of Seven (G7), money and wealth are highly valued. In primitive societies (or social structures), biologically-derived structures of kinship (e.g., clans) are more highly-valued than the U.S. dollar or the Kuwaiti dinar.

In ethics, *value* denotes the degree of importance of something. For instance, food is important and therefore highly valued. Money is important and is, accordingly, highly valued. Love is important, constantly coveted, and highly valued. In marketing, that which is valued is that which satisfies human needs. **Things that are *valued* are normally things that are not only coveted and important, but in many cases, *necessary* for survival.**

Value, in the context here, refers to the aggregate characteristics, properties, or attributes of a person through which a person determines their own usefulness, worth, or desirability. Just as the value of a thing can be determined by *externally ascribed* attributes, qualities, or exchange value—something for which there is a ready market of interested suitors—so, too, can the value of a person with an *ambivalent notion of self* be influenced and determined by external forces external.

If a thing has no worth—even sentimental worth—it has no usefulness, and if a thing has no usefulness or "use-value"—meaning that the thing cannot satisfy a human need or want and is not sought after, desired, or needed—it is considered worthless and having no purpose. If that thing has no purpose, then some might ask, why does it exist?

When human beings determine that something is worthless, useless, and therefore, has no purpose, we ignore it and treat it poorly. We don't care for it, or we discard it. The world is replete with things that are worthless, useless, and serve no purpose, including parts of the human anatomy.

"Value," in the context used herein, refers to the aggregate characteristics, properties, or attributes of a person by which a person determines their own usefulness, desirability, or worth.

Developmental scientist Dorsa Amir, a postdoctoral scholar at the University of California, Berkeley, refers to parts of the human anatomy that no longer serve a purpose as "evolutionary leftovers." Some body parts used to be necessary and useful for human survival, but no longer have such value. This includes the appendix, the palmaris longus muscle (which 10% of human beings no longer have), arrector pili (goose bumps), and auricular muscles in the ear. If these body parts were removed, it would not negatively impact the person's quality of life.

Unless you are a minimalist—a person who focuses on the fewest things needed for comfort, existence, or work— you can probably look around your room and identify things that, if they disappeared today, would not impact you or be missed. And we can all think of commercial products that serve no purpose. Do you remember *Flooz*?

Launched in 1999, Flooz (an Arabic term for *money*) was an alternate form of currency that people could send by e-mail to others, like a gift card. The recipient could then use it to buy things at only a few participating online retailers. I remember seeing one of the many Flooz commercials ($8 million dollars' worth) featuring actress Whoopi Goldberg as their spokesperson, and thinking, "Huh? Why is that needed? Can't I just buy someone a gift card which they can use at *every* retailer, not just Flooz retailers?" The masses seemed to agree. In 2001, just two years after launching, the company filed for Chapter 7 bankruptcy protection.

Self-worth functions similarly. If a person has an ambivalent notion of self, low self-worth, and low self-esteem, and believes they are not worthy of being loved, cared for, desired, or needed, the person will not see their own worth, usefulness, or value. When that occurs, the person could begin to treat themselves as people do to other people or things they find worthless: they will treat them(selves) poorly, they won't care for them(selves), or worse. Conversely, secure, self-validating individuals experience greater success at achieving a sense of *fulfillment*. In this context, fulfillment represents the real or perceived satisfaction of needs, desires, and the attainment of personal and professional aspirations.

While most self-assured, rational human beings seek fulfillment through certain domains, in pursuit of happiness and their definition of life's meaning, that pursuit becomes challenging when people feel intrinsically empty. People with an extremely low sense of self-worth often describe themselves as feeling this way.

When you think about *emptiness*, what comes to mind? I imagine that people conjure up images of a thing or place that is devoid of substance. It is not occupied or inhabited, it lacks activity, it contains *nothing*, or at least nothing of value. On a slightly deeper level, one might imagine a person, place, or thing that lacks value, meaning, or purpose. And this feeling of emptiness—though it implies the existence of *nothing*—can significantly impact the person experiencing the void or sense of intrinsic *nothingness*.

An empty gas tank or dead battery on the highway can induce feelings of fear and anxiety. An empty room can cause disorientation, uncontrollable fear, and panic attacks in people with a condition called *kenophobia*: an intense, irrational fear of empty spaces. Even emptiness in insignificant or meaningless things can cause anxiety, stress, and irrational anger: have you ever been cooking Thanksgiving dinner and realized that you were out of *salt*?

At work, when our heads are empty of thoughts or ideas, our productivity falls and we waste time and work longer hours, negatively impacting our personal well-being. Physiologically, if a person's stomach is empty of food and water, the condition would lead to hunger and malnutrition. Nutritional deficiencies can lead children to develop depression and unhealthy coping behaviors, including eating disorders, substance abuse, and self-harm. In adults, hunger and malnutrition—*emptiness*—can result in diminished muscle, damaged internal organs, and lower bone mass, contributing to chronic diseases, like diabetes and heart disease. When we are *morally* empty or *bankrupt*, we trade away or forget our core values and commitments to ourselves, to institutions, and to others. Put differently, we trade away our self-identity. When we do, our inhibitions diminish and it becomes easier to engage in injurious behaviors to ourselves and others.

Psychologically, it is quite common for people to experience being unfulfilled or empty, a feeling that has been magnified during the Covid pandemic. "Feeling empty" is how many people with low self-worth describe their state, whereas others may use a different term, such as depression, to communicate that something within them is missing. The feeling of emptiness can manifest itself in conditions that are more specifically understood, such as a sense of loneliness, a lack of motivation to pursue anything of significance, and even a sense of feeling lost, similar to that of being lost in the woods. For example, people may report feeling anxious or afraid, not knowing how to get out of "the woods" or where they are going. This feeling of emptiness could be a sign of a mental health condition, like bi-polar disorder or depression. A troubled person might even feel if you are living without a purpose "why live?"

Placing such a negative value on oneself manifests low self-worth. Self-worth determines one's feelings of worthiness, which translates into feelings of usefulness and value. When one feels self-emptiness, it is not unreasonable to associate that empty feeling with a measure of uselessness. And if something is perceived to be useless, it is easier to discard than it is to discard that which is filled (fulfilled) and has value.

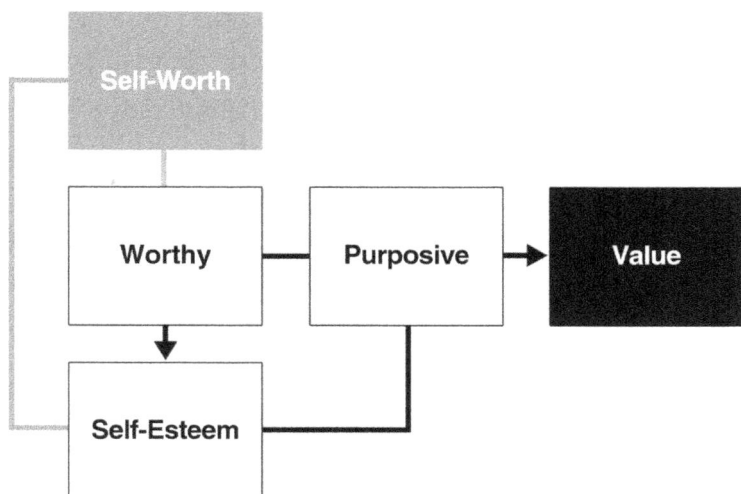

To be clear, it is possible for someone or something that is empty to still have worth and to be useful, with value and a purpose. However, the person's or thing's worth, use, or value may not be perceived or understood by the person themselves, the holder of the item in question. It is like a man who possesses bona fide, societally-agreed upon physical beauty from the perspective of members of that society, but, to himself, the man's low perception of self compels him to believe and act as though he is an ugly gargoyle.

Some years ago, I received two lovely wine glasses as a birthday present. When I unwrapped the beautifully wrapped Bergdorf Goodman gift, revealing two glasses, two thoughts came to mind. First, "Why is each glass individually boxed?" And second, "Why did my friend buy me a pair of *wine glasses*? I don't even drink!"

Although I thought the wine glasses were a wonderful gesture of congratulations and friendship, they nonetheless went straight to the basement onto a storage shelf. There they sat, gathering dust, until a friend of mine recently got married. When deciding on a wedding gift, I remembered the wine glasses and thought they would make a great gift for a couple who drank wine, like my friend and his wife. So, I had the glasses professionally gift-wrapped and gave them to the happy couple. A few days later, my friend called me:

"Yooooo! Thank you for the wine glasses! Damn!" By his reaction, I assumed he *really* liked them. I was happy.

"Hey," I replied, "Nothing's too good for a friend on his wedding day."

"But, damn! You really shouldn't have," he added guiltily.

"No, really, it was no big deal."

"$850 for two wine glasses! That's crazy! But, thanks though, man. My wife and I *love* them!"

After the phone call, I sat there. Silent. Wondering: "What did he mean '$850'?" So, I located the Bergdorf gift receipt, went online, and did a search for the wine glasses. The search result almost made me call my friend and ask for the wine glasses back: *VERSACE Medusa D'or White Wine Glass; $425 each.*

Without having taken the time to understand the exchange-value (cost) of the glasses, to me, as a non-wine drinker, the wine glasses were useless. Because I saw no need for them, I would never use them. This meant they served no purpose to me and had no use-value. Therefore, they were expendable. I put them on a shelf in my dusty basement and disposed of them the first opportunity I had. However, even though the glasses were useless and unnecessary to me, and had no *personal* value, they did, indeed, have *exchange value despite my ignorance.* I could have returned them to Bergdorf for a refund or I could have sold them online.

The fact that I believed the wine glasses had no use or *perceived* value did not truly reflect their **actual value that was unknown to me**. The reality was that the wine glasses *did* have value—significant exchange-value—that my shortsightedness and perception blinded me from realizing. This is often true of people with low self-worth and feelings of emptiness and uselessness. They all possess value, but their value has not yet been intrinsically defined or identified. And, just like me, people act without realizing or defining their intrinsic worth and value, something that *every* human being possesses.

The challenge for many people, especially those with feelings of low self-worth, is to understand their value, believe that they *do* possess it, and that it will be manifested when that value is revealed or presented in the right circumstance.

A person's sense of **worth, usefulness** or **purpose**, and **value** often become evident when the person gains an appreciation for how they connect with others—something for which all human beings have the capacity—and how they can contribute to society and the common good, i.e., their usefulness or purpose.

As British-American anthropologist Ashley Montagu wrote in "Growing Young," children are not only born with the need to be loved—which informs children's mental conception of self—but also the need to love others. Austrian physician and psychiatrist Alfred Adler, the creator of the school of thought known as *individual psychology*, believed that human beings are born with the need to be connected with each other. This connectedness, he proposed, forms a willingness and need to cooperate with others for the common good. Taking the concept further, Thomas J. Sweeney, professor emeritus at Ohio University, concluded:

> The only salvation from the continuously driving inferiority feeling is the knowledge and the feeling of being valuable which originate from the contribution to the common welfare. ... Valuable can mean nothing other than valuable for human society.

The idea that human beings have an innate desire to practically help others is a trait Montagu calls *compassionate intelligence*. Montagu, as well as Adler and Sweeney, generally believe that social interest, connectedness, and the intrinsic need to help (love) others is necessary for feeling worthy and useful (i.e., **valuable**). It is also important for well-being, and achieving life satisfaction.

When people with an ambivalent notion of self come to realize and believe that: (1) they possess intrinsic value, even if their value has simply not been understood by them; (2) their value can be manifested through connections with others who will appreciate the value they bring; and (3) contributing to the good of society in whatever form they are capable, they will likely begin to feel not only worthy, useful, necessary, and valued, but also **significant**.

A person's sense of worth, usefulness or purpose, and value often become evident when the person gains an appreciation for how they connect with others and how they can contribute to society and the common good, i.e., their usefulness or purpose.

SIGNIFICANCE

noun: sig.nif-i-cance | \sig-'ni-fi-ken(t)s \

1. **A subliminal or conscious intrinsic basic need that motivates behavior**

2. **A perception that possesses the qualities of self-worth, feelings of necessity or purpose, and a sense of value**

3. **A mission that is pursued toward personal fulfillment**

SELF-WORTH, VALUE, NECESSITY, AND SIGNIFICANCE

Modern society has shaped the art of making people feel dispensable. Millennials understand belonging to a community as an opportunity to reverse this tendency: pursuing a sense of belonging becomes a means of achieving a sense of being needed."

–SHIRLEY Le PENNE–

That which is *necessary* is essential, requisite, and vital, to achieve a result, goal, or other desired outcome. Because we establish goals based on satisfying that which is physiologically or psychologically required for functional existence, the concept of *need* separates itself from something that is either worthwhile, useful, or even has value.

Human beings need food for our ultimate goal: survival. I say this is our *ultimate* goal because, faced with the choice of dying today and going to "the great beyond," or doing anything else, healthy, rational people will choose to live. To accomplish the most desired human goal of survival, what do human beings actually *need*? Fundamentally, we need food, we need water, we need air, sunlight, and, to a degree, we need protection from the elements of nature, including such things as fire, clothing, and shelter.

Maslow proposed that humans *require* the elements in his Hierarchy of Needs, while more contemporary thinkers in the field, such as neuroscientist Dr. Nicole Gravagna, believe that, in addition to food, water, and shelter, human beings need sleep, human connection, and *novelty*, which he defines as the opportunity to learn and the potential to fail. The test for *necessity* is to ask: If we voluntarily removed the thing in question (e.g., water), could the thing under consideration (human life) proceed? Based on the question of survival, could a person live without self-actualization, electricity, the wheel, or the Phillips head screwdriver? If the answer is "yes," though these things might have tremendous *value*, they are not *necessary* for survival.

The test for *necessity* is to ask: If we voluntarily removed the thing in question (e.g., water), could the thing under consideration (human life) proceed? In the question of survival, could a person live without self-actualization, electricity, the wheel, the Phillips head screwdriver? If the answer is "yes," though the thing might be of tremendous value, it is not "necessary" for survival.

Taking an example from the physiological and psychological realms to the physical, the same test of necessity applies to work, goods, services, work occupations, and even individuals: Is the mail carrier useful? Yes. Is s/he valuable? Yes. It is a great service to have mail and packages delivered directly to your front door. Is the mail carrier *necessary*? No. If there were no mail carriers, people would still be able to get their mail and packages, albeit more inconveniently. What about the church pastor? The doctor? The same rationale would apply. The necessity of a doctor or surgeon is a tricky one, given the changes in the way human beings have become accustomed to living over the centuries. Modern humans cannot imagine a world without such medical professionals. However, modern human beings with the capacity for language survived without trained doctors for approximately 100,000 years; more, if you consider homo sapiens dating back more than 300,000 years. As Thomson, et. al. explained in "History of Medicine:"

> Magic and religion played a large part in the medicine of prehistoric or early human society. Administration of a vegetable drug or remedy by mouth was accompanied by incantations, dancing, grimaces, and all the tricks of the magician. Therefore, the first doctors, or "medicine men," were witch doctors or sorcerers.

THE ISLAND QUESTION

To more easily conceptualize the nuance between that which is useful, valuable, or necessary, consider this question: Which would you prefer to take with you on a hazardous journey into the wilderness: (a) something that you find to be *useful*; (b) something that you believe has (situational) *value*; or (c) something that you will *need* on such a journey?

As with most things of interest to human beings, satisfying our distinct, basic needs not only drives our behavior, but is also the reason why we develop goals or aspire to a desired outcome. For instance, if a person is hungry, it is an indication that the person has a physiological need that must be satisfied. To satisfy the physiological need—hunger, in this case—s/he sets out to get something to eat to satisfy that need. So, to "stave off hunger" becomes the purpose or goal the person establishes for satisfying their physiological need that manifests as a feeling of hunger.

To function optimally, fundamental needs must be satisfied. This is a truism for human beings, animals, businesses, and other organizational forms. By the same logic, if a person's goal was to survive a hazardous journey into the wilderness, I suspect that most rational people would choose option (c) from the choices above, in other words, something that is *needed*.

Suppose you were stranded on a deserted island with only the clothes on your back: a t-shirt, a pair of khaki pants, and a pair of flat boat shoes. You know nothing about the island: who, if anyone or anything, inhabits it; if there is food or a viable water source; if there is any form of shelter, anything. More importantly, you do not know when or if a boat or airplane will be coming to rescue you from the island.

With that as a premise, if you could take any three (3) things onto that deserted island with you—from the table below—which three things would you take?

Which 3 Items Would You Take?	
• A box of 250 matches	• An inflatable life raft
• A crate with 24 bottles of water	• A compass
• A bottle of rum	• A flashlight (solar)
• A warm blanket	• A mirror
• A first aid kit	• 15 feet of nylon rope
• Your mobile phone (no charger)	• A fishing kit
• An axe	• 24 Snickers bars
• A gun with six bullets	• Shark repellant
• A water desalinator	• A flare gun

Initially, when I asked this question without providing a person with any options, their choice of items would vary wildly. I once conducted a job interview with a college sophomore who said that she would take: her cell phone ("So that I can text my friends to tell them where I am"), a copy of *People Magazine* ("In case I get bored. I couldn't *live* without my *People Magazine!*"), and a pack of breath mints ("In case I run into someone on the island"). Now, whenever I ask this "island" question of anyone, I provide them with a list of options, if for no other reason than to move the dialog forward.

The most commonly-chosen items that people *initially* elect to take onto the island with them are: 24 bottles of water, a flashlight, and a gun. Admittedly, there is no perfect group of three choices or answer to this question. I also understand and acknowledge that limiting the choice to only three items doesn't seem to be enough to survive on an unknown island. However, there is a purpose for limiting the number of items a person can take with them: the "scarcity" effect.

Scarcity suggests that there is only a finite amount of resource available to satisfy infinite needs. When this is the case, a person faced with a scarcity of resources necessary to satisfy a basic need will develop a *scarcity mindset*, whereby the person's decisions and behaviors will be dictated by the fact that there is a scarcity of the resource. The scarcity mindset will force people to become singularly-focused on the need for which there is a scarce resource that is required to satisfy the need. For example, if a group of people is faced with starvation and the food supply is limited—and not enough to stave off every group member's hunger—the starving people will eat *anything* that is available, not leaving a scrap of food or a crumb on their plates after licking it clean. The people's minds will be preoccupied and singularly-focused on food. At that point, long-term thoughts and plans go out the window and their obsession becomes the here-and-now: "How can I satisfy my hunger *today*?"

To reiterate, resource scarcity makes people think tactically as opposed to strategically or longer-term, as they might when resources are abundant. If a family of four is financially wealthy, their thoughts might be focused on how they can invest their extra disposable income to have a better retirement in 20 years, or how to buy securities so that they can pay $305,000 for four years of their kids' college tuition at New York University (NYU). This family with abundant financial resources can think long-term, about the future. Conversely, it is not uncommon for a middle-class family of four earning $53,000 per year to figure out how to stretch $75 until their next paycheck in two weeks. Money scarcity will dictate that the middle-class family's thoughts become laser-focused on how they can feed their kids *now*, this week. Paying for the kids' college in five years is not that important right now. Pressing needs—for which we set goals to satisfy—limit long-term perspective.

Scarcity also forces people to make trade-off decisions. The middle-class family with only $75 to last them for two weeks will inevitably be forced to make a trade-off between responsibilities: Do they use the money to buy food for the family, get new tires for the car, or do they pay the electric bill? These scarcity-driven decisions will force the family to decide between that which is useful, desired, or *needed*. In this example, a rational family will conclude that the car tires, while they would be nice to have, are not a necessity at the moment. Paying the electric bill is important, and electricity is valuable for computer usage, television, having lights, and running the refrigerator. But the kids **need** food or they cannot function, or worse, they could become seriously ill. The family will choose to spend the money on food which is physiologically **necessary**, as opposed to new car tires which would simply be nice to have.

Useful	Valuable	Necessary (For accomplishing your goal)
Car tires	Electricity	Food and water

This is the idea behind The Island Question: Scarcity of resources—the person can only take three things onto the island—will (*should*) force people to focus on their **goals** and to figure out how to act *tactically* to accomplish them. If a person's goal is *to survive on the island for some length of time in hopes of being rescued*, the person will choose a related set of items that will help them survive for a long period of time. If the goal is to get off the island as quickly as possible, the choices will be different.

Because of the scarcity of options, the person whose goal is to survive on the island for as long as possible will then have to decide which of the available items are absolutely **needed** to accomplish that goal, versus which items are simply nice to have. Sure, a warm blanket would be nice to have and a fishing kit would be very valuable to a person stranded on an island with no food. Ultimately, however, while the blanket and fishing kit would be quite useful, they are not truly necessary. The sorting of available items might look like the table on the next page.

People have an intrinsic, fundamental desire (i.e., need) to be as worthy, valued, and needed—*useful, valuable*, AND *necessary*—as are water, food (snickers), fire (matches), and an axe in this scenario.

OPTIONS	Useful	Valuable	Necessary (for your goal)
A box of 250 matches	●	●	●
24 bottles of water	●	●	●
A bottle of rum			
A warm blanket	●		
A first aid kit	●	●	
Your mobile phone			
An axe	●	●	●
An inflatable life raft	●		
A compass	●		
A flashlight (solar)	●	●	
A mirror	●		
15 feet of nylon rope	●	●	
A fishing kit	●	●	
24 Snickers bars	●	●	●
Shark repellant			
A flare gun	●	●	

When it comes to deciding what is truly necessary, the decision is normally based on what will satisfy an important fundamental *need*, like water, for example, and not a "want" or a "nice to have," such as a compass or blanket. In certain contexts, they do have use-value. However, in the island context, they are relatively *insignificant*: too unimpactful or unimportant to be worthy of consideration for satisfying your goal of survival.

I have discussed the value that group and community affiliation can provide to members through their participation in these social structures, including enhanced feelings of belonging and worth. In addition, the *feeling of being needed* creates a sense of *indispensability* and worthiness, strengthening one's notion of self, leading to feelings of self-respect and significance.

The feeling of being needed creates a sense of indispensability and worthiness, strengthening one's notion of self, leading to feelings of self-respect and significance.

SIGNIFICANCE

If *insignificance*, as I define it, refers to something that is too unimpactful or unimportant to be absolutely necessary for accomplishing a person's goals, then **significance** can be defined as that which *is* absolutely needed. Understanding and defining my concept of *significance* is like understanding and defining a *common cold*.

A common cold, as defined by the Mayo Clinic, is "a viral infection of the nose and throat." It is a combination of several upper respiratory tract symptoms, including: a runny or stuffy nose, sore throat, cough, congestion, slight body aches or a mild headache, sneezing, and a low-grade fever. Significance, as I propose, is something that possesses—in varying degrees—implicit or explicit qualities of worth, usefulness or *purpose*, value, and necessity. In that respect, it is like the common cold—a combination of qualities and attributes—and also like other life missions and purposes, in the sense that these aspirations are not just a singular concept. Achieving a purpose, for example, requires that several "things" be achieved for that purpose, mission, or goal to be satisfied.

Something or someone that is significant will not be discarded as useless, unimportant, or *insignificant*. Rather, they will be coveted, valued, loved, and considered to be of the highest importance.

Significance differs from Maslow's need for "self-actualization." Whereas self-actualization is a fundamental intrinsic need for self-fulfillment, understanding, and achieving one's own potential, significance is a **status** and **intrinsic knowledge**—whether subliminal or conscious—that possesses the qualities of **self-worth**, a **sense of value**, and **feelings of necessity**, to varying degrees. Another major difference between the two is that self-actualization is highly aspirational and may never be achieved in one's lifetime, whereas significance is realistically and commonly achievable to varying degrees. Self-actualization and significance are similar, however, in that both can be pursued as a life mission, purpose, or goal, and they can be subliminally pursued. Subliminal pursuit of a mission, purpose, or goal occurs when a person's actions and behaviors are instinctive, on auto-pilot in a sense, and directed toward achieving the qualities of significance, even though the person may not have specifically, outwardly defined a goal *to achieve and maintain significance.*

Pursuing significance is not contingent upon satisfying lower level physiological and other human needs as proposed by Maslow, nor is it mutually exclusive from pursuing other life goals. For example, if a person's life mission is *to be a public servant and a champion to those who do not have the means or wherewithal to defend or advocate for themselves,* or *to own a successful neighborhood pizza parlor* intrinsically, at their core, they will also want to achieve significance through these other, conscious life missions.

All human beings want to have positive self-worth, to be valued, and to be needed, whether they are poor and hungry or financially wealth. Significance drives a person from within and emanates from their inner self.

Significance, as I propose, is something that possesses—in varying degrees—the implicit or explicit qualities of worth, usefulness or purpose, value, and necessity. In that respect, it is like the common cold; a combination of qualities and attributes.

My proposition is that Significance is the foremost manifestation of self-worth, the pursuit of which is a fundamental, core psychological need.

Something or someone who is significant will not be discarded as useless, unimportant, or insignificant. Rather, they will be coveted, valued, loved, and considered of the highest importance.

At the beginning of this chapter, I discussed the concept of need and necessity. Specifically, I focused on that which is necessary to accomplish the fundamental human goal of survival. Living. *Physiological* needs. Current research is being conducted to better understand the value of *psychological* and *neurobiological* needs as motivators for behaviors to accomplish holistic, mental-health-, and well-being-related goals.

Psychologically, *need* is a feature that motivates a person to act to accomplish a goal, just as with physiological need. It guides behavior, giving it purpose. This is consistent with Maslow's theory that all human behavior is motivated by a hierarchy of needs: physiological, security, social, esteem, and self-actualization. Psychological needs, however, differ in their motivation to satisfy needs that are not biologically necessary, such as those essential to mental health.

In his 2007 book "Neuropsychotherapy: How the Neurosciences Inform Effective Psychotherapy," German psychotherapeutic researcher Klaus Grawe proposed that there are four psychological needs that motivate human behavior: attachment; orientation and control; pleasure maximization and pain minimization; and the need for self-enhancement. I will focus on the latter—self-enhancement—given its relevance to this topic.

Self-enhancement (or *self-esteem enhancement*) is the intrinsic *basic need* to strengthen, *enhance*, maximize, and protect our self-esteem. In strengthening and protecting self-esteem, people will behave rationally or in an extreme, pathological way if that is what the person believes is required to protect their self-esteem. It is worth noting, however, that, while people are motivated to satisfy basic needs, enhance self-esteem, and accomplish goals, our behavior is sometimes intentionally counter-productive to achieving those ends.

Physiological and psychological basic needs, such as self-enhancement, are related. As human beings look to satisfy basic needs, the pursuit of satisfying physiological needs, for instance, can be thwarted by the pursuit of satisfying psychological needs, if the person determines psychological needs are more important. This phenomenon is referred to as *low self-esteem maintenance*, in which the person purposefully engages in behaviors that maintain low self-esteem related to one goal, to use the effort to service needs related to a more important goal. Ultimately, the person determines that the tradeoff is worth it, because the reward of pursuing the more important goal exceeds that of the sacrificed goal. For example, a business person might conclude that *turning down* a managerial promotion—a career-goal that would bolster self-enhancement and esteem—would afford the person more free-time for family, friends, hobbies, and self-care, which the person values much more than the promotion and the accompanying two-percent raise. Ultimately, these decisions are still geared toward maximizing self-esteem and self-enhancement.

The Self-Esteem Enhancement Conflict

Protecting self-esteem can not only maximize it, but it can also be problematic for a person with a low opinion of self, lacking in self-assuredness or confidence. Maximizing or enhancing self-esteem often necessitates *improvement*, which requires transformation. All improvement requires change. If a person has a fragile ego due to an ambivalent notion of self, they will resist change for several reasons. First, if they have a fragile ego, they may consider the need for improvement as an insult or threat to an existing domain on which they base their self-esteem. If so, the person will resist change. Second, if the person lacks confidence and self-assuredness, the notion of change can be intimidating, leading the person to find comfort in their existing paradigm and resist change. As humans, we are predisposed to the status quo, for self-preservation.

Change can be difficult since its impact is often uncertain. It is an unknown, so our initial reaction is fear! It is common for people to resist change because of this fear and the perceived risk associated with the unknown. If I change my sucky job and get a new job that will enhance my self-esteem, will the unfamiliar new job be worse than my current, known, sucky job? What If I am bad at the new job and I get fired? That's a risk. These possible negative consequences frighten me.

Fear is one of the most powerful human emotions, because it can prevent people from engaging in activities that could be in their best interest. In addition, fear has an evolutionary benefit in that it fuels a safety instinct—for example, being naturally fearful of approaching a lion—and to improve our current condition, such as, becoming more knowledgeable to qualify for a better job that will not only enhance my self-esteem, but also lift my family out of poverty. On the down side, however, fear can keep us from making the necessary changes to achieve our goals and become the best that we can. Fear is one of the most significant obstacles to maximizing self-esteem and achieving personal success.

A colleague of mine, philosopher Bobby Lee Smith, says that *we fear things in direct proportion to our ignorance and lack of understanding of them.* With this as a premise, any activity for which we have no experience—and therefore, little understanding—is somewhat fear-inducing. When people are asked to make changes, we are often being asked to do something with which we have no experience and no knowledge, resulting in fear-induced resistance. Therein lies the conflict:

- People are intrinsically motivated to strengthen self-worth and enhance self-esteem;
- Self-esteem enhancement requires strengthening or improving a domain of self-worth;
- Upgrading self-esteem requires change;
- Human beings fear change, and therefore resist it; so,
- We forego any opportunity to enhance and strengthen self-esteem and improve self-worth.

SELF-ENHANCEMENT AS A BASIC NEED

Dehumanization

I believe that feelings of worth, value, and significance are core, fundamental human needs. They signify *humanity*, the acknowledgement that we are human and, therefore, worthy of love, belonging, and kindness. It means that we are a valued part of society, the human collective, the human race, and not simply things, machines, or animals. We are not "less than," but, instead, equally-valued.

Unfortunately, around the world, some human beings are *dehumanized*, whereby perpetrators perceive others as less humane or overall "less than" themselves. Perpetrators use this rationale for anything from denying others their humanity (e.g., the American period of African enslavement), to perceiving others as robots and excluding them from the category of being *human* (e.g., Chinese factory-workers), or stigmatizing groups as lacking human sensibilities (e.g., women and the homeless). When they do this, it becomes easier to marginalize entire groups of people.

The perpetrators' dehumanizing perceptions and behaviors lead to the targets of dehumanization *feeling* dehumanized. When they do, they begin feeling that their fundamental, basic human needs—not to mention human *rights*—are trampled upon, leading to *self-dehumanization*: negative feelings of a lack of belonging and being less worthy, which influences their notion of self, self-worth, and self-esteem enhancement.

For these reasons, I find value in the arguments by Grawe; clinical psychologist Dr. Gregg Henriques, author of "A New Unified Theory of Psychology;" researchers Edward Deci and Richard Ryan, whose Self-Determination Theory proposes that humans have *"fundamental universal psychological needs* that are essential for growth;" and others, that human beings have a fundamental, core psychological need to maximize self-worth and self-esteem. One of the major challenges to strengthening one's notion of self, maximizing self-esteem enhancement, and protecting feelings of significance is what I refer to as **Value Impediments**.

Value Impediments

In the context of this book, *significance* is defined as that which possesses the qualities of **worth**, **value** (which embodies usefulness and purpose), and **necessity**. Significance, I propose, is the foremost manifestation of self-worth, the pursuit of which is a fundamental, core psychological need.

SIGNIFICANCE		
Worth	**Value**	**Necessity**

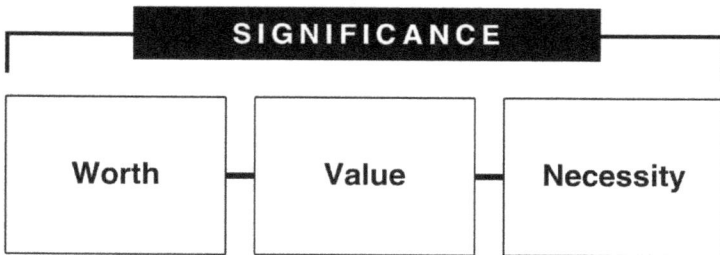

Complete significance is like *perfection*. Although everyone wants to achieve it, we can never do so completely. Perfection suggests a state of flawlessness, without defects. People who desire perfection do so to overcome their perceived inadequacies, minimize their shortcomings, and compensate for their deficiencies. They may also do this because they fall prey to our culture's unachievable definitions of what the ideal or "perfect" person should be, do, have, or look like. Think about the unattainable images on social media. This is consistent with my definition of perfect or *complete* significance.

Complete significance refers to a state of achieving a perfect notion of self and self-worth, and a sense of being 100% useful, valuable, and necessary. While it may be possible to achieve completeness in some aspect of significance—such as worth, purpose, value, and necessity—it is unlikely that a person can achieve completeness in all of them. In this sense, complete significance is like perfection; we all strive for it, but can never achieve it. The reason is because we all have insecurities that diminish our notion of self, our sense of self-worth, and self-esteem. Plus, we cannot control how external factors influence our sense of self-worth. Knowing this, we spend our lives pursuing complete significance, while subconsciously knowing that we will never achieve or attain it. However, like perfection, there is value in achieving some degree of significance and there is also value in its pursuit.

> In 1959, during his first team meeting as the coach of the Green Bay Packers football team, legendary championship-winning coach Vince Lombardi, after whom the National Football League's Super Bowl championship trophy is named, instructed: "Gentlemen, we will chase perfection, and we will chase it relentlessly, knowing all the while we can never attain it. But, along the way, we shall catch excellence."

Suppose, for example, that Joe's self-worth is derived from his appearance, which is his basis of self-esteem. The first question that comes to mind is: How does Joe define the standard of a good "appearance?" Who defines attributes of "appearance?" If *externally*-defined, why should Joe concede that *that* person's definition is not in itself flawed, incomplete, and imperfect, thus rendering Joe's appearance incomplete or imperfect itself —assuming he conforms to the person's completeness or perfection attributes?

If Joe's standard of appearance is in any way externally-defined—as is everyone's standard of *acceptable* appearance to some degree—then he will never achieve
it, if for no other reason than external definitions of
things like beauty, style, and appearance are subjective,
whimsical, and are influenced by, among other things,
the times in which a person lives—meaning that it is
also *relative* and not absolute. For example, if you asked
a person to define a female standard of physical perfection in 19th century America, the person would likely
describe someone Rubenesque: pleasantly rounded or
having a physique associated with Flemish painter Peter Paul Rubens' female portraits. In the 21st century,
however, the preference seems to be for women on the
slimmer end of the spectrum. So, the 19th century ideal
was relative to that period, but by today's standards,
that is not generally the case. Even still, there are mil-
lions of men and women whose idea of a "perfect" body
is closer to that of a Sumo wrestler than it is to Lolo
Jones' physique; it's subjective and relative. What is
considered to be a great "appearance" today will likely
change, just when Joe has become comfortable with his
adherence to the now-outdated standard of appearance.

Unfortunately, Joe may never realize that he cannot
achieve 100% completeness in the *appearance* basis or
domain of esteem, because, to some degree, it is based
on externally-defined standards over which he has no
control. Audrey Lorde would likely say that Joe is not
defining himself for himself. If he did, he would have a

greater chance of achieving positive feelings as he meets his *intrinsically-defined* standards of a great appearance, than he would by trying to live up to the *other-defined* standards.

As one pursues significance—self-worth maximization—they are constantly confronted by experiences that challenge and detract from a domain in which one stakes their own self-worth and significance. In this context, a *domain* is an experience or attribute on which one bases their self-worth. For example, if Ken bases his self-worth and feelings of significance on being financially "rich"—however he defines *rich*—then *monetary wealth* would be a domain on which Ken bases his self-worth.

In the course of everyday life, people are confronted with experiences and situations that detract from their notion of self, their feelings of worth, and ultimately, their sense of *value*. Someone or something which has no value is perceived as worthless, useless, insignificant, and therefore, disposable.

Suppose that Ken, from the previous example, lost half of his wealth investing in the stock market. The loss would negatively affect his monetary wealth—a domain in which he staked his self-worth—thereby impeding or preventing his ability to achieve his version of significance.

An *impediment* is something that slows, delays, or prevents someone from accomplishing an important goal by obstructing their progress toward succeeding in their domain(s) of self-worth and esteem. Worthiness and usefulness/purpose contribute to one's sense of value. Without feeling valued, one cannot achieve a sense of necessity or, consequently, significance. Therefore, in the pursuit of significance, attaining a sense of *value* becomes a *critical success factor* (CSF): an element that is necessary for a person to successfully accomplish a goal, such as, achieving monetary wealth and ultimately, significance. Put differently, without establishing an intrinsic notion of being valued—the CSF for success—one cannot achieve significance.

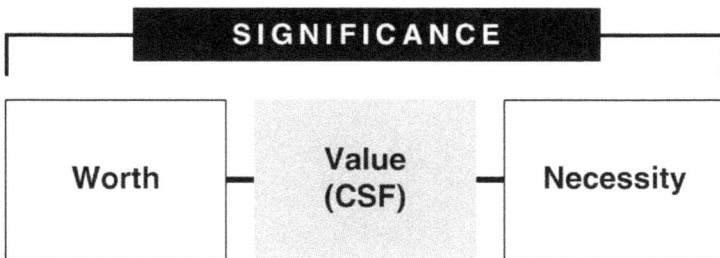

SIGNIFICANCE		
Worth	Value (CSF)	Necessity

A **value impediment** is anything that interferes with or obstructs a person's ability to achieve success in a domain in which the person stakes their self-worth, self-esteem, and significance. This is the so-called *domain of significance.*

PART THREE

A POSTULATE

THE POSTULATE OF SIGNIFICANCE

My *postulate of significance* supposes that, as people try to increase and protect their notion of worth, self-esteem, value, and necessity for the purpose of achieving significance, they experience a *self-esteem enhancement conflict*. When they do, they defend their self-enhancement to the degree that they may act irrationally if the **threat to their self-enhancement and value is an impediment to a domain of significance**. Psychologically, our behavior is driven to satisfy intrinsic and core needs, such as self-enhancement, to reach an end or goal. In doing so, we either act in a rational way or an extreme, unacceptable, pathological way if we are presented with a self-esteem enhancement conflict. If my self-esteem enhancement is contingent on being "right" about a position I have taken on a controversial issue—even though evidence shows that my position is wrong and, internally, I agree that it is wrong—I will lie and cheat and defend my position with irrational anger to protect my reputation (prestige) and defend my self-enhancement.

Examples of pathological behaviors that can result from a threat to a domain of significance, like prestige, include: lying, cheating, exaggerated actions, relationship relapses, causing harm to oneself and others, irrational anger, and racism, to name a few.

Examples of pathological behaviors that can result from a threat to a domain of significance, like prestige, include: lying, cheating, exaggerated actions, relationship relapses, causing harm to oneself and others, irrational anger, and racism, to name a few.

DOMAINS OF SIGNIFICANCE

I define a *domain of significance* as an area of interest or life that one pursues in hopes of strengthening the notion of self toward achieving significance. The pursuit of success in the domain drives behavior intended to satisfy success requirements in the domain. Achieving success in a domain of significance increases feelings of self-worth which contributes to one's sense of value and necessity, eventually resulting in an intrinsic notion of having significance—something to which we all aspire. For some, achieving and maintaining significance becomes a *subconscious* life purpose or goal; they might not be consciously aware of the pursuit, but, nonetheless, it drives them on an instinctive level.

My interest in understanding what drives the irrational behavior of otherwise healthy, sober, well-adjusted, and rational human beings led me to identify five general domains of significance that, if threatened, substantially influence people's irrational behavior. These domains of significance are:

1. **Validation**
2. **Prestige**
3. **Respect**
4. **Desirability**
5. **Preeminence**

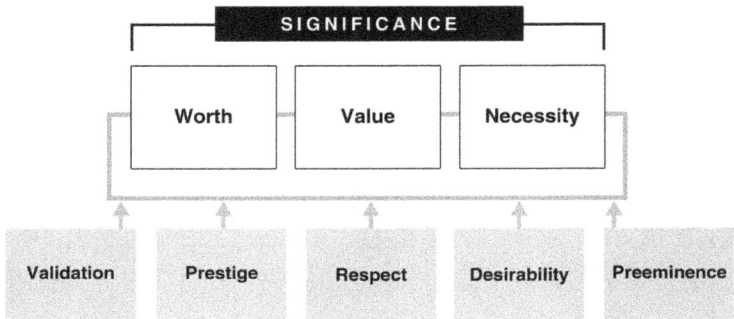

Human insecurity threatens achievement in a domain of significance. Most people experience feelings of self-doubt, a lack of confidence, being undeserving, and simply not-up-to-par at some point in life, while others feel insecure all the time. Whether our insecurities arise as a result of past rejection, feelings that one doesn't belong in the crowd in which one finds oneself, past failures, or being "imperfect"—flawed, possessing defects, not our dream-self—the fact remains: everyone feels insecure at some point, and some more than others.

Human insecurity detracts from or thwarts success in a domain of significance, often leading people to behave irrationally to guard the domain and counter the feelings of insecurity to protect the self and self-esteem. In that sense, **human insecurity is an impediment to significance**.

Imagine that you are THE bigshot in your hometown of Deadwood, South Dakota, home of the 1876 Gold Rush with a population 1,300. People love you, look up to you, and want to be just like you. You make a very good living, earning $135,000 per year, three times the median household income in Deadwood.

Because you are a bigshot, a friend told you about an event that would be right up your alley: the annual *Wall Street Journal* Live conference, at a total cost of more than $5,000 per person. To top it off, the friend held an invitation to the invitation-only event and offered it to you. You decide to attend to hobnob with "other" bigshots like you. You believe that attending the conference would bring you even greater adulation and respect when you return to Deadwood. After all, guests at the event include celebrities, like Academy Award-winning director James Cameron and top-level executives, such as Apple CEO Tim Cook. Hanging out with such a prestigious crowd would certainly bring more status-by-association.

So, you throw on your best South Dakota finery and fly to Laguna Beach, where the event is being held. As you arrive at the venue in your Uber, you notice that the crowd—who all seemed to arrive in stretch town cars, Rolls Royces, and Cadillac Escalades—seemed much different than *you*, but similar to each other. The men walked around with an air of arrogance, as though they ruled the world, and the women, each adorned with at least $50,000 in jewelry, reminded you of Eunice "Lovey" Howell, the rich socialite on the 1960s TV show Gilligan's Island. You felt out of place. During the event, all the other attendees seemed to know—or wanted to know— the other important-looking attendees, but no one wanted to know *you*. Imagine how insecure you would feel in this social setting. This would shake anyone's confidence and detract from their sense of prestige, respect, and self-esteem.

A Value Impediment (VI) negatively impacts the achievement of significance by decreasing one's sense of worth and self-esteem, or feelings of value and necessity, all of which contribute to, detract from, or thwart one's goal of achieving significance.

An increase in a domain of significance enhances one's intrinsic and external perception of value, while a threat or decrease to a domain can have the undesirable, opposite effect of decreasing the perception of value and impeding progress toward achieving significance. Plus, there can be tradeoffs: if there is an increase in one domain and a decrease in another, the net difference between the two state-changes will act to improve or reduce one's ability to realize significance to a degree.

An increase in a domain of significance enhances one's intrinsic and external perception of value, while a threat or decrease to a domain can have the undesirable, opposite effect of decreasing the perception of value and impeding progress toward achieving significance.

The following example explains the concept further. Suppose that Abby, a very confident and accomplished woman, believes her level of significance to be at a "10," which is *complete* significance, the highest level achievable. The level numbers used in this example—to quote actor and comedian Drew Carey as he explained the point-scoring system of his '90s ABC improvisational comedy "Whose Line is it Anyway?": "The points are just like soap in the men's room. Doesn't matter."

Each time that one of the five domains of significance is impeded, the resulting impact is a *reduction* in the level of an associated quality of worth, value, or necessity, all of which negatively impacts Abby's notion of significance. Conversely, any increase in a *domain* of significance *positively* impacts significance. In Abby's case, impediments to success in three of her domains of significance—against only one positive impact—results in an overall net decrease of "two," reducing her perceived significance level from a "10" to an "8."

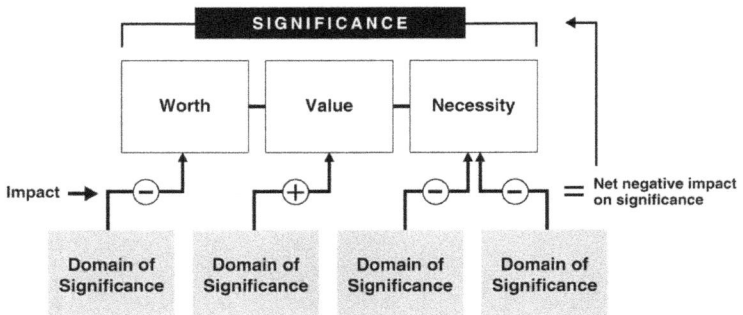

★

Each time that one of the five domains of significance is impeded, the resulting impact is a reduction in the level an associated quality of worth, value, or necessity, all of which impacts one's notion of significance. Conversely, any increase in a *domain* of significance has a positive impact on the perception of significance.

Returning to the Deadwood, South Dakota bigshot scenario, the social setting at the *Wall Street Journal* Live conference would have awakened feelings of insecurity, negatively impacting the bigshot's prestige, preeminence, and respect domains of significance. The result is a lesser sense of self, decreased self-esteem, a lesser sense of value, and consequently, feelings of being less significant and important.

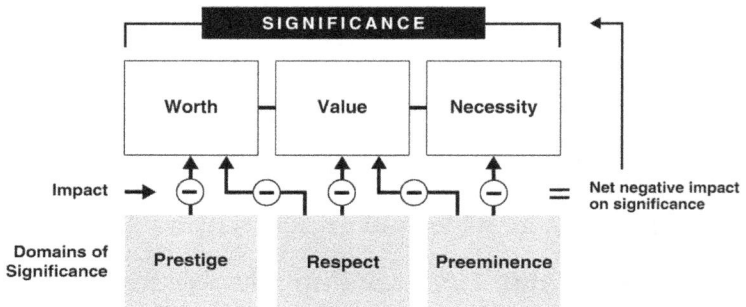

AN EXPLORATION of THE DOMAINS of SIGNIFICANCE

and examples of how rational people behave irrationally in pursuit of success in each domain

THE FIVE DOMAINS OF SIGNIFICANCE

I. VALIDATON

"Queen of social chameleons, I mastered the art of telling people what they wanted to hear and being someone they would find impressive—all the while worrying incessantly about what others thought of me, fearing criticism, and holding myself back as a result."

–Sacha Crouch, *psychologist, and author*

Validation is the desire—and in some cases, need—to have others approve of your behavior or like and agree with what you say, do, or believe. Validation-seekers, approval-seekers, and people-pleasers behave in a way to make others feel good. They receive satisfaction when their often disingenuous approval-seeking behavior complies with the expectations of others and elicits praise and adulation from their intended audience. When they receive the desired response, dopamine—a brain neurotransmitter that is active in the brain's intrinsic reward and pleasure centers and provides the sensation of pleasure—is administered which, to the validation-seeker, feels like a drug. The insecure feel approved, validated, and better about themselves.

From an early age, most people are taught that we must behave in a polite, friendly, appeasing way to make others feel good. For instance, African-American men were often taught to appear as non-threatening as possible when entering an elevator that had a white woman as its only other occupant. Th reason was that, traditionally in America, white women—especially older white women— felt threatened being alone in an enclosed space, such as an elevator, with a black man. Even though the woman's fear is irrational and racist, it is the black man who must behave non-threateningly (i.e., irrationally) to make the women feel good, safe. Knowing that the woman feels safe puts the man at ease and he feels validated, even though he has done nothing that should have made her feel uneasy in the first place.

Receiving praise and adulation can be intoxicating, so the more we seek validation, the more we condition ourselves to behave in a way that elicits a positive response from others. Eventually, as a salve to calm our insecurities, we train ourselves to readily engage in those behaviors that get us the most positive responses.

The need to be liked, approved of, or validated—a trait we acquire as children when we depend on others for our care and establishment of worth—is a characteristic of low self-esteem and contingent self-worth. Low self-esteem can drive validation-seekers to abandon their integrity, behave disingenuously, outright lie—to themselves and others—and even behave irrationally to receive approval and to be liked.

EXAMPLES OF VALIDATION-BASED IRRATIONALITY

Kevin Doesn't Know, But Serena Does

During the 2016 Summer Olympics in Rio de Janeiro, Brazil, Women's National Basketball Association (WNBA) player and U.S. women's basketball center Brittney Griner, a 6'8" 205-pound force on the court, told *USA Today* that she would love to play against National Basketball Association (NBA) and U.S. men's basketball player, 6'10" 275-pound center DeMarcus "Boogie" Cousins. "I would love to just go out there and play against (Cousins)," said Griner. The reporters then asked other members of the U.S. men's basketball team what they thought of such a matchup. When asked his opinion, Kevin Durant, arguably the greatest basketball player in the world today, scrunched up his lips and looked sideways, as if to say, "What kind of ridiculous question is that?" But then something interesting happened: Durant said, "I like the confidence [Brittney Griner], but I don't know if that's gonna happen." Upon hearing Durant's answer, I thought: "Really, KD? You don't 'know' if Brittney Griner would beat Boogie Cousins in a basketball game?"

Cousins is one of the fiercest, strongest, meanest, hardest-to-stop centers in the history of the NBA. When he power-dunks, other big NBA players move out of the way to avoid injury. His strength and athleticism are impressive, even against other large men in the league. Incidentally, he is two inches taller and outweighs Griner by 75 pounds. Griner's athleticism? Although Griner can certainly dunk a basketball in-game—in 13 years in the WNBA, she has dunked 23 times—her vertical leap is, at best—assuming she is in the 95th-percentile of all women—estimated to be 19 inches; 7.5 inches less than that of Cousins. Griner is used to playing against other WNBA players with an average height of 6'0." Cousins plays against men in the NBA whose average height is 6'8," the same as Griner's. You get the picture: for Griner, playing against Cousins and winning would be a monumental ask.

Other players and coaches were more forthright in their response to the *USA Today* reporter's question. Legendary coach Luigi "Geno" Auriemma, head basketball coach of the University of Connecticut's women's basketball team that has won 11 National Championships, was more honest in his response: "If there's no referee, I'm gonna go to the ATM, and I'm gonna sell my house, and I'm gonna put all my money on DeMarcus Cousins."

Yes. I know the question was a light-hearted one, and I am sure that Durant wanted to be inoffensive with his answer. However, it was obvious by his initial eye-roll and facial expression that he believed the question was not a serious one, knowing that such a game would be a mismatch. We can surmise that Durant and Auriemma felt similarly about the possible outcome, but, unlike Auriemma, Durant chose to be disingenuous. But why would a self-assured, rational person do that?

I suspect that, had Durant given the answer which his facial expression implied, he would have said something like, "That's ridiculous. Next question." But, is it possible he thought that such an answer would potentially make WNBA players and women in general think he was being sexist, which could influence his likeability and sense of worth? So, to give an acceptable answer, he chose to knowingly lie to himself and signal that he is not sexist, thereby protecting the *validation* and *respect* domains of significance.

This is a clear example of *approval-seeking* behavior, being so concerned with the opinions of others and how he would be perceived that he chose to give an inoffensive answer. Instead of being forthright, like Auriemma and fellow NBA player Draymond Green—who, after looking surprised by the question responded, "I got [Cousins] on that one"—Durant gave a safe answer that was inconsistent with his true feelings. Durant's answer could also be considered an example of *socially-desirable responding*, defined as: "The reluctance to admit unpopular beliefs or behavior to avoid making a negative impression."

It is possible that Durant lied to be gentlemanly, to protect Griner's feelings and not affect her self-esteem, a lie that is considered an *other-oriented* lie. Such behavior is understandable, but no less irrational. Other-oriented lying can also be considered selfish, because it is done to protect Durant from taking responsibility for any disappointment Griner might feel from his response. People's natural behavior is to present themselves as an amiable, acceptable person to others. Or, as proposed by researchers DePaulo et al, in their paper *Lying in Everyday Life*:

> " ...the portrayal of everyday lies as disruptive of social life and hurtful to the targets of the lies is in need of modification. In keeping with the perspective described by ... social interaction theorists, we think that many of the lies of everyday life are told to avoid tension and conflict and to minimize hurt feelings and ill-will."

Research also shows that people are more likely to tell other-oriented lies to people they are close to, whereas they tell harsh truths to people not known to them. This seems to be the case with Durant's response. He could be thinking that, sometimes, other values matter more than total honesty. However, studies also show that people usually want to know the truth, whether it is good or bad, positive or negative. When people are forthright and honest, the truth-teller (Durant) earns trust, respect, and credibility from the victim (Griner), which not only strengthens their relationship with each other, but also increases Durant's sense of worth by positively impacting the significance domains of validation and respect of others.

For some, however, like former American tennis champion John McEnroe, who has never been accused of lacking in self-confidence or feelings of insignificance, honesty is the best policy.

During a June 2017 interview on National Public Radio (NPR), McEnroe said that Serena Williams, arguably the best pound-for-pound tennis player ever, was the "Best female player ever. No question." He then went on to say, "If she played on the men's circuit, she'd be like 700 in the world." Williams responded on Twitter: "Dear John, I adore and respect you but please please keep me out of your statements that are not factually based."

McEnroe's comments caused backlash. The next day, he appeared on *CBS This Morning*, hosted by Norah O'Donnell, Gayle King, and Charlie Rose. Rose opened by saying, "Let's start with the elephant in the room: Why was it necessary ..." McEnroe interrupted, "What do *you* think? Charlie, you're a tennis guy, you like to play tennis, I see you on the tennis court. What do you think Serena would be ranked if she played in the man's game?" Rose answered, "I have no idea. But she seems pretty strong to me." "Very strong!" McEnroe agreed, "The greatest female player ever."

After the volley between Rose and McEnroe, O'Donnell asked McEnroe directly, "Would you like to apologize?" "Uh, no," he replied matter-of-factly.

It could be argued that Charlie Rose honestly didn't know the answer to McEnroe's question, when he responded, "Nobody can prove this," or Rose believed that Williams would surely be ranked higher than 700, though not #1. Or he hedged to be more liked and approved by those who disagreed with McEnroe's stance.

What is interesting is that, more than four years before McEnroe made his controversial comments on NPR, Serena Williams appeared on "The Late Show" with David Letterman in August 2013. They discussed the famous 1973 "Battle of the Sexes" tennis match in which top women's player Billie Jean King, 29, beat Bobby Riggs, 55, who boasted that women were inferior, and that he could beat any female player. Letterman then asked Williams, "What would happen if that occurred today?" Serena replied, "[British men's champion] Andy Murray's been joking about myself and him playing a match. I'm like, 'Andy. Seriously. Are you kidding me?' To me, men's tennis and women's tennis are completely almost two separate sports. If I were to play Andy Murray, I would lose 6-0, 6-0 in five to six minutes. ... The men are a lot faster, they serve harder, they hit harder, it's just a different game."

"Thank God"

I have often wondered why people routinely repeat the now clichéd refrain "I want to thank God," at every public opportunity possible. There are a few things that puzzle me whenever I hear the phrase uttered by someone who won an award, a boxing match, or a football game; and, it is always said by the victors. We never hear: "I want to thank God for our 49-0 loss to the lowly New York Jets."

Of all the things that puzzle me about the refrain, the thing that baffles me most is: Why are they thanking God in the first place? Sure, I know that Jesus said, *"It is written, 'You shall worship the Lord your God, and him only shall you serve.'"* (Luke 4:8). But *why* shall people worship him? John Chapter 4 Verses 23-24 states: *"But the hour is coming, and is now here, when the true worshipers will worship the Father in spirit and truth, for the Father is seeking such people to worship him. God is spirit, and those who worship him must worship in spirit and truth."* But still, there is no reason given for why God is "seeking such people to worship him," other than the fact that God is seeking it. But *why*?

A rational free-thinker would ask, "If God is all-knowing and all-powerful—the mightiest force in existence—why would God need people to worship him? (Note: I am using the pronoun "him" in reference to

God since this is the most commonly used pronoun in this regard. I acknowledge that God could be a *him* or a *her* or even an *it*, because a *person* cannot be a God, can they?)

I tried to imagine that *I* was all-powerful and all-knowing, like a God. I have the power to do anything ... *anything*! I know everything, billions of religious people fear me, I never need for anything. I am considered perfect. So why would I care if someone worshiped me or thanked me after winning a boxing match? I don't suppose I would get mad if no one worshiped me; I'm God! I am not human, so I don't have human emotions like anger—although God did say, "*You shall not bow down to them or serve them, for I the Lord your God am a* jealous *God.*" (Exodus 20:1-26). *Jealous?* That's a story for another day.

But, if I am an almighty God, I know what everyone is thinking and I know which of the people who incessantly thank me are frauds and disingenuous. I can heal people; I can decide who gets sick; I can help one football team defeat another team—which, according to the number of football players who thank me, I must do quite often. I can feed everyone on the planet and I can even eradicate sickness and poverty. I know what everyone is going to do *before* they do it—including *thanking me*. So, it is irrational to believe that an infinite, omnipotent God would *need* feeble mortals to thank him. Kings and rulers crave deference and thanks because they are human and have human **insecurities**. They need to feel appreciated and preeminent. But *God?*

Even though theists believe that God is omniscient and knows everything that is and will be done throughout the universe, and that God is omnipotent—all powerful—people still have free will. So, since God is a *God* and has no human emotions (let's ignore Exodus for the moment) like anger and vengefulness—*anger* implies that the omniscient God didn't know something would or would not happen against his liking, causing God to be angry—a God could not be pleased, humbled, grateful, big-headed, or flattered by a person thanking him. It is unnecessary. Plus, since the person's free-willed actions led to their accomplishment, such as winning an award, what role did God play in these actions? The only non-conflicting answer can be "none." Otherwise, if God helped the person win an award or the sporting event—therefore understandably deserving thanks—then the person does not have free will, and God picks winners and losers. Is it rational to believe that?

If I am an almighty God, I know what everyone is thinking and I know which of the people who incessant thank me are frauds and disingenuous about their complete adherence to my scriptures. I can heal people, I can decide who gets sick, I can help one football team defeat another team—which, according to the number of football players who thank me for helping them defeat the opposing team, I must do quite often. I can feed everyone on the planet and I can even eradicate sickness and poverty. I know what everyone is going to do before they do it—including thanking me. So, it is irrational to believe that an infinite, omnipotent God would need feeble mortals to thank him.

I am sure all religious people and God-thankers know this about God, so why do they use every public forum to unnecessarily (in my opinion) thank God out loud—and then wait for the applause? If people believe that God will get angry at them if they don't thank him for everything, then they don't believe that God knows what they are thinking, what they really feel inside, whether or not their thanks is genuine, whether they are appreciative of their fortunes, or that, as a God, he is without human emotions—with all due respect to Exodus 20:1-26. Put differently, they don't truly believe he is a *God*, in the strictest sense of the word.

Try to imagine it: *You* are a God, not a human being. You are in all parts of the universe, you know more about everything than anyone who has ever lived, you need nothing, you never get tired, you can snap your fingers—metaphorically—and make every American begin speaking Mandarin just for kicks. You have no human emotions, such as anger, because you know everything that is going to happen and you control everything, so if you foresaw that the impact of someone's free will was undesirable, you could change it. You are never sad, happy, depressed, stressed, sick, or vulnerable; you are a God! With this as a premise, why would you care if some mere human who is on earth for only a relative nanosecond thanked you when they won an award?

My opinion is that people publicly say "I want to thank God" to garner positive feedback and praise.

That approval-seeking behavior is not intended to win favor from God—it is ignorant to think that this is even possible—but is instead intended to influence how the God-thanker is perceived by the audience. They want to be liked. They don't really *want* to publicly thank God; to do so is simply irrational. Instead, I believe that—under the influence of sodium thiopental (i.e., truth serum)—they would admit that thanking God is their way of saying to the audience, "I want you to think I'm a good person and to like me."

My *significance* postulate would consider such God-thanking behavior an attempt to enhance self-esteem by earning cheap praise, kudos, acceptance, and validation which would make the God-thanker feel good about themself. Perfunctory God-thankers possess **contingent self-worth**, which means their intrinsic notion of self and their worthiness of love and caring comes from the adulation and approval of others, not from within themselves. True, lasting self-worth only comes from within.

Approval-seeking, need-to-be-liked syndrome, and people-pleasing are all attempts to find self-worth from the approval of others through lying. Lying, in this sense, is a form of manipulation that allows the God-thanker to tip the crowd response toward adulation. Think about it: In America, have you ever heard anyone *boo* after someone said "I want to thank God?" For God-thankers with contingent self-worth, thanking God becomes a defense mechanism to protect themselves from being disliked or invalidated, from being vulnerable and insecure.

A person cannot lie to themself, which means that any adulation one receives from disingenuously thanking God will ultimately be muted by the intrinsic understanding that the adulation was manipulated and not received genuinely, based on truth. Such lying that is told in the God-thanker's own interest is called **self-centered lying**, lies told to manipulate others into making the liar feel better about themself. Plus, when we lie, we inflict unhappiness on ourselves through devaluation.

In an article entitled *Verbal and Nonverbal Communication of Deception,* researchers Zuckerman, DePaulo, and Rosenthal describe lying as a form of deception, where deception is defined as "an act intended to foster in another a belief or understanding which the deceiver considers false." Put differently, gratuitously thanking God to receive adoration is an act that the God-thanker performs to make the audience believe something about them (e.g., that the God-thanker is a good, God-fearing person) which the disingenuous God-thanker knows is not true.

A rational response would be to give thanks to the real, actual people who supported you in accomplishing the feat for which you are giving thanks—those who would feel honored, appreciated, and valued by the recognition—rather than God, who, if he is like me-as-God, already knows if you genuinely want to offer praise, but who finds it unnecessary and irrational to do so—whether disingenuously or perfunctorily—just so that people will like you more.

As Nobel Laureate George Bernard Shaw wrote in "The Quintessence of Ibsenism:" "The liar's punishment is, not in the least that he is not believed, but that he cannot believe anyone else."

II. PRESTIGE

"The easiest way to be bigger than yourself
is to lie."

–Penn Jillette, *American magician*

By definition, *prestige* is the widespread **respect and admiration** felt for someone or something based on a perception of their achievements or quality. Originally, however, prestige was more akin to Penn Jillette's comment than this more conventional, positive definition.

The root of the word *prestige* comes from the Latin word *praestigum*, meaning a trick or delusion. Over time, prestige developed a more positive connotation: highly-regarded, accomplished, upper-class, a highly-coveted status, something or someone to be respected and admired.

We all strive to achieve prestige in some aspect of life. Because, to do so would mean we would have achieved some form of success (however we define it), the respect of others, a status achieved by few, and, in the nomenclature of Abraham Maslow, *self-actualization*. Put differently, if we achieve prestige, we will have achieved an added degree of *significance*. However, as you may imagine, the pursuit, maintenance, and defense of prestige-associated significance can cause one to behave irrationally.

EXAMPLES OF PRESTIGE-BASED IRRATIONALITY

Gidget

In the closing scene from the 1959 film "Gidget," starring Sandra Dee as Francine "Gidget" Lawrence and James Darren as Jeffrey "Moondoggie" Matthews, the brand-new couple head to the beach on the eve of Moondoggie's departure for college. After a big kiss, he says to Gidget:

"Oh, gee. Would you, uh, sorta wear this 'til I come back?" He then reaches into his pocket, retrieves his high school pin, and pins it onto her sweater.

"Oh, *boy* would I!" she replied, excitedly. "Oh, just wait! Wait 'til the girls get a load of this! Honest to goodness it's the absolute *awesomest!*"

Of the myriad possible thoughts that could have been running through Gidget's head, her first thought was, "Wait 'til the girls get a load of this?" It sounded as if she wanted to brag about her pinning rather than invite "the girls" to share a happy moment in her teen-aged life. Her reaction seemed as if she was saying, in effect: "You older, more worldly girls looked at me as the younger, naïve, sheltered little sister with no sex appeal, but look what *I've* got: Moondoggie!"

This assumption requires an explanation. Early in the movie, sweet, innocent, flat-chested,16-year-old tomboy Gidget was invited to go to the beach with her well-developed older school friends. They tried to teach her how to get the attention of the surfer boys, but to no avail; she wanted to surf instead. So, the older girls left the hapless Gidget on the beach and went "man-hunting." But soon, Gidget-the-lost-cause landed one of the most popular, desired boys of them all: *Moondoggie*! This is why I believe it is fair to imply that she wanted to say, "Look at me now!" She wanted to **brag**.

Bragging—saying things boastfully—is consistent with the original concept of *prestige*, namely boasting. People talk with excessive pride and self-satisfaction (i.e., brag) about their possessions, achievements, successes, abilities, and anything else that will garner the respect and admiration of those to whom they brag. I believe that bragging is a manifestation of one's insecurities, and that people brag about things in a domain in which they feel insecure or incomplete, as if they are trying to fill a void. It is possible that people who brag about being engaged—or pinned, in the case of Gidget—are insecure about their desirability, being worthy of love.

As psychologists Robert Wicklund and Peter Gollwitzer wrote in their research entitled *Symbolic Self-Completion, Attempted Influence, and Self-Deprecation*:

> "A concept of symbolic self-completion states that people define themselves as musicians, athletes, etc. by use of indicators of attainment in those activity realms, such as possessing a prestige job, having extensive education, or whatever is recognized by others as indicating progress toward completing the self-definition."

It could be argued that people who brag, boast, or show off are doing so to fill in that which is missing in their intrinsic notion of self. One may intrinsically *believe* they are worthy of receiving love, but they may not totally be convinced. Something is missing. So, they try to fill the void—that which they feel is missing—by receiving confirmation from others related to the incomplete part of the self about which they feel insecure. Sometimes, completeness does not come through simply being admired, but the perpetrator (i.e., braggart) feels the need to position themselves one step above those in a target group. In Gidget's case, the target group was her worldly friends.

This behavior suggests that the insecure person is completing their definition of themselves through others, rather than for themselves.

Bragging, boasting, showing off, rubbing it in, exaggerating, lying, or any other term used to describe the approach people use *for the sole purpose* of seeking and receiving the admiration and praise needed to make themselves feel important, prestigious, worthy, valued, and significant, is irrational. And nothing speaks more of irrational prestige-seeking than the diamond engagement ring, or the high school pin in Gidget's case.

I specifically call out *diamond* engagement or wedding rings because no one brags about getting engaged and then shows off their $25, thin-as-a-toothpick, gold-plated, I'll-upgrade-it-when-I-get-some-money engagement ring. No. Women only want to show off (i.e., brag about) their *diamond* rings. And not just any ol' diamond ring, but only those that are one carat or larger. I am using "women" receiving rings from men in this scenario due to tradition. That said, women receive rings from other women, and men often receive diamond engagement rings from men and women, too.

It seems that when a woman becomes engaged and the fiancé spends the recommended two to three months' salary on the engagement ring, irrational behavior ensues on the part of both the woman and the man.

The De Beers Group, the world's leading diamond company, specializing in everything from diamond mining to diamond trading, proposes that, as a general rule, you should spend at least two months' salary on the engagement ring—*pre-income-tax*. So, if a man's annual salary is $120,000 per year, he should spend $20,000 on an engagement ring. This, to me, is irrational. First, no ring of any type is needed to become engaged, let alone one that costs $20,000. Second, is it rational for a man to spend $20,000 on something that is coveted, yet unnecessary, when that same money could feed an impoverished African village of 100 for an entire year? Third, there is no correlation between the amount of money one spends on an engagement ring, how much one person loves another, and how long a marriage will last. Case and point: Rapper and producer Kanye West spent $4 million on a 15-carat diamond ring for Kim Kardashian. Their marriage ended after approximately 6.5 years. Now, take a look at a couple—*any* couple—who has been married for 50 years. Look at the woman's ring: modest, nothing to brag about.

According to the Gemological Institute of America (GIA), the idea of the engagement ring began in 200 BCE. It was given to a woman as a business contract or the affirmation of love and *obedience*. In 850, the ring came to symbolize a man's intent to marry and make a financial sacrifice, since rings were now made of gold. This begs the question: Why did the man need to demonstrate financial sacrifice? Whatever the reason was it was likely irrational. Today, according to *Brides Magazine*, the bible of all things wedding-related, the necessity of an engagement ring—a "somewhat outdated wedding tradition"—has been called into question. They write that commitment itself is what's important, not the jewelry attached to it. They even suggest several creative tips for proposing without a ring, including such gems as: proposing with a tattoo, a pet, or a movie stub from your first date.

However, the fact that none of these alternatives will stand as a welcomed surrogate for a diamond ring for most women illustrates the irrationality of expensive diamond engagement rings. While I believe that an engagement ring is an unnecessary gesture to demonstrate one's love and commitment, I also acknowledge the reality that proposing to a woman by giving her a parakeet, for instance, would do more harm than good in the self-esteem department.

A 2017 HuffPost article entitled "Why Are Women So Insecure?" proposed that one reason for women's insecurity is because *many women have learned how to validate themselves through a man's approval of them.* Presenting a woman with a huge diamond engagement ring is a sign to the woman that she is loved, coveted, worthy of care, and has her suitor's approval. These feelings help strengthen the woman's notion of self, feelings of value, and significance. Conversely, giving her a parakeet would likely have the opposite effect. Plus, the diamond ring will provide the woman with another opportunity to strengthen her feelings of self-worth and prestige by showing off her beautiful big ring to her single friends and those with smaller rings. Showing her friends a $20 engagement *parakeet* would likely bring ridicule, reducing the woman's feelings of worth, prestige, and significance.

Both behaviors by the engaged woman—showing off her big ring but hiding the engagement parakeet—are irrational. If she received the diamond ring, she will use it to garner praise and admiration, making her feel superior to her friends and filling a void in her notion of self. If she received the parakeet, she would be embarrassed to show her friends because of the *opinions* they might form about her and her taste in men, arousing her insecurities. What gets lost in each of these scenarios is the fact that a man has expressed his love for her, asking her to be his wife and spend her life with him. To the insecure woman, that's not what is most important at that moment. The $20,000 ring—the beautiful admiration-inducing prop—is what matters. Utterly irrational.

★

Both behaviors by the engaged woman—
showing off her big ring but hiding the
engagement parakeet—are irrational. If
she received the diamond ring, she will
use it to garner praise and admiration,
making her feel superior to her friends
and filling a void in her notion of self.
If she received the parakeet, she will
be embarrassed to show her friends
because of the opinions they might form
of her and her choice in men, arousing
her insecurities, thus missing the point
of becoming engaged.

The engaged *woman* is not alone. Buying an expensive diamond ring also provides *the man* with an opportunity to earn validation and prestige. Presenting the woman with an expensive ring will make the man feel liked and appreciated by the happy woman. He will appear considerate, generous and impressive to her friends, and it will also make him feel good about himself. This tri-level feedback will bolster the man's validation: "We wish we had a man like him;" admiration: "It cost *how much*?!;" and a sense of value: "I made her so happy!;" all while filling a void in the man's sense of self.

This behavior is similar to the behavior exhibited by men who spend $1,400 on a decidedly unappealing designer shirt, such as the Gucci *Green Musixmatch Edition Bowling Shirt*; it is irrational. The primary value the items possess is convincing people to admire the owner or believe that the owner has prestige. I call such behavior irrational because spending $20,000 on an unnecessary ring or $1,400 on a bowling shirt, only to use it as a status symbol and create a false illusion that will counter-balance the owner's insecurities, is illogical and insensate.

These displays of self-absorption are not confined to diamond engagement rings and designer clothing. Instead, admiration-seeking behavior is displayed by people across all walks of life, such as:

- Professional athletes who unashamedly describe how they fritted away their first million dollars. In 2020, GQ Sports, a brand of *GQ Magazine*, created a video series called "My First Million," where 30 well-known professional male athletes described how they spent the first million dollars they earned after signing a professional contract. The athletes squandered their money on such excesses as a $500,000 car, $370,000 on clothing, and $50,000 on a night out in Los Angeles. What's even more irrational is that the 30-episode series featured only two white athletes; the others were Black or African-American (26!) and Latino (2), many of whom came from impoverished backgrounds. Such behavior supports research that suggests people from underserved communities and those not in the majority often feel the need to go to extra lengths, often irrational, to gain the perception of prestige.

- Former President Donald Trump claiming: "I have the best words," "I am the best builder," "I have a very good brain," "Nobody's ever been more successful than me," "I know more than the generals," "Nobody reads the bible more than me," and many, many, more.

- Entertainer John Edward trying to convince vulnerable people that he can communicate with the dead.

- People who boast and name-drop about the famous or high-profile people they know, met, hung out with, have bedded, took a photo with, or have as a relative. By associating with other admired, prestigious people, the name-dropper hopes to increase their own admiration from others by what I call the **transference of association.** Here people hope some of the earned-admiration of the famous person transfers to them, thereby earning the name-dropper admiration-by-association. As psychologists Robert Cialdini, et al., proposed in the *Journal of Personality and Social Psychology*, people hope to achieve self-enhancement by associating one's self-publicity (i.e., boasting) with successful others.

The *transference of association* occurs when people hope to achieve self-enhancement by associating one's self-publicity (i.e., boasting) with successful others.

"I am D.B. Cooper"

In November 1971, a man identifying himself as "Dan B. Cooper" purchased a one-way ticket with cash, and boarded an airplane in Portland, Oregon for a 30-minute flight to Seattle, Washington. Once airborne, Cooper—who would later become infamous as "D.B. Cooper"—handed a flight attendant a note, which she ignored, prompting him to whisper into her ear, "Miss, you'd better look at that note. I have a bomb." D.B. Cooper was hijacking the airplane. He demanded $200,000 in cash, four parachutes, and a fuel truck on standby in Seattle to refuel the aircraft in preparation for its rerouted flight to Mexico, per Cooper's order.

When the flight arrived in Seattle, Cooper allowed the other 36 passengers to exit the plane, but he kept some of the flight crew on board. Later, when the flight neared Reno, Nevada, Cooper opened the airplane's rear hatch and parachuted into infamy. To date, D.B. Cooper has never been found, although, periodically over the years, some of the money and various clues have surfaced, but to no avail. D.B. Cooper's hijacking remains one of the great unsolved mysteries in FBI history.

The legend of D.B. Cooper has turned the hijacker into a folk hero to many people. He got away with it! Several books, documentaries, podcasts, articles, and movies have been produced, each presenting theories of how he must have pulled it off, assuming he survived the airplane jump. With each story, the legend grows, creating legions of D.B. Cooper fans around the world—people to whom he is fascinating, even admired. He is now so admired, in fact, that several people have claimed to *be* the outlaw.

Over the past 50 years, no fewer than 13 people have either come forward claiming to be D.B. Cooper or alleging they have evidence of who he is or was. D.B. Cooper claimants include a wide range of people from varying backgrounds, including a transexual woman, several military and World War II veterans, and an accountant, among others. This creates a dilemma: either all 13 of the purported Coopers colluded to pull off the amazing crime, or as many as all of those who are alleged to be Cooper or have confessed are lying. They can't *all* be D.B. Cooper. So, as it relates to significance, if one of them actually *is* Cooper, then why would the other non-Coopers claim to be the hijacker? The same question would apply to any other notorious imposter, such as: Murderer Christian Karl Gerhartsreiter, who posed as "Clark Rockefeller," a supposed member of the wealthy American Rockefeller family; and Anna "Delvey" Sorokin, a scammer who posed as a wealthy German heiress and New York socialite. What force is so strong that it compels people to take the enormous risk of living as another person, someone of greater stature than their real selves, knowing that, at some point, their true identities will be uncovered and the consequences of their charade could be serious? There are several potential reasons, including self-enhancement, seeking prestige to increase significance, or even narcissism.

The excessive need for admiration is a characteristic of *narcissistic personality disorder.* Because narcissists have a fragile sense of self-worth, often feeling worthless and insignificant, they constantly need to be admired by giving others the impression that they are superior, have more "stuff" than others, and are special. A construct that characterizes the needs and wants of narcissists and those who desperately seek prestige is *fame.*

Research on **fame** and one's sense of self (e.g., "social self:" one's self in relation to others) suggests that prestige- and fame-seekers believe in self-importance. They are preoccupied with the need to be accepted by others, to be valued by others, to be perceived as being superior to others, as well as with the need for status. Fame and its associated status, admiration, and prestige give the prestige-seeker a heightened sense of their social-self, enhancing feelings of worthiness, being valued, and significance.

The excessive need for admiration is a characteristic of *narcissistic personality disorder*. Because narcissists have a fragile sense of self-worth, they constantly need to be admired.

III. RESPECT

Respect is something to which all human beings are initially entitled. That is, people should, as a starting point, take seriously the way others present their "self" and the fact that they are human beings. One can also have respect for things, such as a respect for plant life, the law, and the environment. However, there are other bases on which the respecter can have respect for an individual, such as characteristics that warrant positive appraisal by the respecter. For example, an individual might earn respect by being charitable, having integrity, being moral, athletic prowess, or for a high degree of intelligence. Respect based on such characteristics is referred to as *appraisal respect*, which is respect that is more earned than conferred upon one at birth.

Having respect and being respected by others is important for one's notion of self and self-identity. Respect means that others have regard for one's *worth*. Those with positive notions of self come to learn that, by respecting *themselves*, others recognize them as deserving of respect. Feeling respected and experiencing respect from others (e.g., how one is treated by others) can impact one's quality of life and their psychological and physical well-being.

Research presented in *Why the Psychological Experience of Respect Matters in Group Life: An Integrative Account* by Hou and Binning suggests that being respected is a manifestation of one's need for status and belonging, which can, in turn, shape self-esteem. They write that: "The emerging field of the psychology of respect has demonstrated that perceived respect plays a critical role in shaping not only group dynamics but also the individual's emotional experiences and *self-construal*."

Disrespect, or even the lack of receiving respect, relates to an individual's insecurity about belonging, leading to an increase in the need to strive for superiority, and general feelings of inferiority. *Minderwertigkeitsgefühl* is the German word meaning feelings of inferiority, a feeling of having *diminished* worth or of being of *lesser value*. Feelings of inferiority could compel people with a low sense of self to behave in a manner that is not only self-promoting, but also irrational.

So, while respect plays an important part in shaping one's notion of self and subsequent feelings of worth, *disrespect*, on the other hand, can have the opposite effect on one's sense of self and self-worth. It can cause the recipient of the disrespect to experience fear, shame, anger, and self-doubt, negatively impacting worth and self-esteem. When a person's need for respect is not met or when the person is disrespected (i.e., treated discourteously, rudely, inconsiderately, or dismissively), the implications can be significant. In addition to the disrespected person's status within a social group being reduced to, in some cases, insignificance, feelings of disrespect can lead to retaliation or violence as a means of regaining respect and restoring lost status. Studies show that in some marginalized communities where respect is highly valued as a sign of significance, the less respected an individual feels, the more likely the person is to respond with irrational, violent behavior.

Research by Anderson, Kraus, Galinsky, and Keltner entitled *The Local-Ladder Effect: Social Status and Subjective Well-Being*, published in *Psychological Science*, proposed that happiness in life is more related to respect than to one's wealth: "Sociometric status—the respect and admiration one has in face-to-face groups (e.g., among friends or coworkers)—has a stronger effect on subjective well-being than does socioeconomic status."

EXAMPLES OF RESPECT-BASED IRRATIONALITY

It's Gotta Be the Shoes!

In November 2012, Western Kentucky University senior Cheryl Williams attended a party at the Gillespie Club in downtown Louisville. According to witnesses, Williams accidentally stepped on a man's shoe—something to be expected at a 1,000-person party—and an argument ensued between Williams and several men. There was no fighting, just arguing. Suddenly, a shot was fired, striking Williams in the torso. The single shot was fatal.

To many, this type of pathological behavior on the part of the shooter is not new. I recall back when I was in high school attending a house party in a rough Philadelphia neighborhood. A friend of mine accidentally stepped on another guy's sneaker. As irrational as it sounds, stepping on someone's shoe in tough, underserved neighborhoods like that where the party was being held is a sign of disrespect. Sometimes, a simple apology will resolve the issue. In this case, however, there were lots of people around who saw the "infraction," including the "victim's" friends and several girls. This meant that the "victim" could not let the incident slide with just an apology. His reputation was at stake. His friends were asking him, "You just gonna let that pussy step on your foot like that?"

People started gathering around, sensing a fight about to break out. My friend apologized, "Sorry, man. My bad." However, that was not good enough. The "victim" went into theatrical mode: "What the fuck is wrong with you? I should fuck you up!" "Take it outside," one of his friends instructed. As they headed to the door to go fight, the party's host suddenly became a peacemaker and convinced the guys to get back to the party and forget the incident. Such let-bygones-be-bygones peacemaking was possible back then, but if it happened today, it is not hard to imagine that a gun might have been drawn.

In a 2020 interview on "VLAD TV," DJ Vlad, the host, shared a story with rapper BG Knocc Out about a fellow rapper named Saigon. Vlad said that he, "Just interviewed Saigon, and he told me about an incident where ... somebody bumped into him. So, he said, 'Yo, you bumped into me,' and the guy was like, 'I don't give a fuck.' [Saigon] pulled out a gun, shot that guy, and accidentally shot another guy that was just in the area. He got six years for that shooting."

BG Knocc Out added, "That used to happen a lot. People stepped on your shoes. People took that shit very seriously. It's the street mentality. In the street, that might warrant you being shot or beat the fuck up real bad."

In such an environment more than in others, people typically lack material wealth, so their **reputation becomes their value**. It denotes their worth. Disrespect is one thing that can decrease one's standing in the community, so respect is coveted, maintained, and guarded as one does with their self-enhancement. Protecting one's status (reputation, respect, worth, and value) can lead a person to behave irrationally or even pathologically.

In such an environment more than in others, people typically lack material wealth, so their reputation becomes their value

I'm Right, You're Wrong

In 2015, Randy Gregory, a former standout defensive end for the University of Nebraska football team, was entering his first year as a professional after being drafted by the NFL's Dallas Cowboys in the second round. Gregory was a sure-fire first round (i.e., one of the first 32 players selected) elite talent, but slipped to day two of the draft because of "character concerns."

Reports of marijuana use and immaturity had dogged Gregory since his days at Nebraska. He missed three pre-draft meetings with The Cowboys, and speculation began about the reasons why. He went undrafted in round one—a big disappointment to Gregory and his family.

In an interview with Jon Machoda of *The Dallas Morning News*, Gregory stated that, "I think a lot of people are getting tied up in the weed and think it's just a weed problem. I don't think it's a weed problem. ... I want to prove everyone wrong."

Gregory's hope to "prove everyone wrong" is not an uncommon desire, especially among athletes, many of whom have been told at some point that they couldn't do this or that, or that they simply weren't good enough. Some people take it a step further by stating, "Nothing brings me more *pleasure* than proving people wrong."

Why is it that so many people—especially athletes—set about to "prove people wrong" as a goal, or derive so much satisfaction from proving people wrong? The answer is they have been disrespected by being doubted, which negatively impacted their sense of self, worth, and value. To the "disrespected," the only way to gain or earn back the respect of the doubters and restore their feelings of self-worth is to **prove themselves to be right** about their self-perception of quality and talent. This allows them to get revenge on doubters by saying "I told you so!"

Yes, proving people wrong, i.e., getting revenge, is not just about respect, but also about demonstrating superior knowledge to the doubters. This earns the person a modicum of prestige—one of the domains of significance. When the doubted is proven to be right, their achievement strengthens their notion of self, increasing worth, esteem, and value. Also, being *right* makes us feel good about ourselves, and when we feel that sense of *accomplishment*, we get rewarded by the brain releasing dopamine, which gives us a pleasure sensation, like a drug. In fact, the dopamine high can be so intense it can motivate or even addict people to constantly seek out the behavior that earned them the dopamine release: being right and others being wrong about an issue. So, it is no wonder why people get so much satisfaction out of proving themselves right: "I love proving people wrong" or "Nothing brings me more pleasure than proving people wrong."

The desire or need to prove oneself right or others wrong is irrational. A person's sense of respect, quality, value, and significance should not be contingent on other people, specifically, other people being wrong, thereby making the person right. It is logical and rational for people to rely on themselves for their own happiness and satisfaction, and not to derive it from the failures or dictates of others. For Randy Gregory, his self-knowledge that he did not have a "weed problem" and demonstrating as much *through his actions* over time—not through his hopes to prove someone wrong—would not only organically demonstrate (prove) it to the naysayers, thereby earning or regaining their respect, but also reinforce his sense of self.

The psychological experience of respect is necessary for one's well-being and for their notion of self. A lack of respect, or worse, *disrespect,* can negatively impact one's sense of worth, value, and significance. However, it has to be earned through one's direct actions, not via words or by setting a goal of "proving people wrong."

A lack of respect, or worse, *disrespect*, can negatively impact one's sense of worth, value, and significance.

IV. DESIRABILITY

I previously wrote that it is through our relationships and interactions with others that humans develop a mental conception of the *self*: our beliefs about our worthiness for care and lovability. For people in late or post adolescence, the need for belonging and lovability becomes more significant than at any other time in life since infancy. Is there any greater feeling than falling in love?

For many, love can be more nourishing than food. Andreas Capellanus wrote in "The Art of Courtly Love:" "He whom the thought of love vexes, eats and sleeps very little." Similarly, in the play "Hamlet," William Shakespeare wrote: "What is a human being if he just eats and sleeps? Nothing more than a beast."

How do you describe what you are feeling when you say you are *in love*? In that sense, being in love is like happiness: you can't really explain what it is or what it feels like, but you know it when you experience it. An interesting thing about love is that, although no one can really describe it—since, I believe, love is an individual experience that differs from person-to-person—different people will describe it differently. I imagine, however, that when people describe being in love, they all agree on one thing: it makes them feel great. When loved, people feel **desired**: attractive, wanted, needed, worthy, valuable; simply put, *significant*.

To Maslow, belonging, romantic love, and general affection are characteristics of *fundamental social and emotional human needs*, or "Love Needs." Maslow theorized that, if a person's physiological and safety needs are fairly well-gratified, then the need for love, affection, and a sense of belonging will emerge. A person will noticeably feel the absence of friends, or a partner, or a spouse, or children. S/he will hunger for affection from people in general, for a place in a group, and s/he will strive—often irrationally—with great intensity to achieve this goal. The person will want to achieve this more than anything else in the world and may even forget that once, when s/he was hungry, s/he didn't give love and affection even the slightest thought.

When loved, people feel desired:

attractive, wanted, needed, worthy,

valuable. Simply put: *significant*.

Psychologist Robert Sternberg proposed a theory called "The Triangular Theory of Love" that describes various stages and types of love, and conditions for each one. He described love as a combination of intimacy, passion, and commitment. Various conditions are proposed to help distinguish the numerous stages and types of love. For example, he describes "Consummate Love" as: "The complete form of love, representing the ideal relationship toward which many people strive but which apparently few achieve." "Romantic Love" is a state wherein "lovers are bonded emotionally (as in liking) and physically through passionate arousal." And "Infatuated Love" is "... often what is felt as 'love at first sight.' But without the intimacy and the commitment components of love, infatuated love may disappear suddenly."

Irrespective of how one defines or describes "love," one thing remains consistent: feeling it or being in it makes people feel desired and significant; and lacking love leaves us longing for it, with "a certain inborn suffering." In that respect, love, as a fundamental human need that is required for well-being, is like food and water; without it, our body and mind tell us that we need it. And research shows that, without love—or, specifically, one of its manifestations—*affection*—human beings cannot function optimally.

Affection has been described as an interchange between two people, where each person gives and receives positive contact and interaction at all times. While affection is more than physical touch, that aspect of affection—and love—is a base human need. Affection deprivation happens when a person does not receive affection. This is also referred to as *skin hunger*.

"Skin hunger" is the biological need for human touch, which explains, for instance, the reason that prisoners in solitary confinement are mentally affected.

They need human contact. This deprivation affects the human mind in several ways, including leaving a person feeling lonely, highly-stressed, unhappy, depressed, and unhealthy. Beginning at birth, human beings have a need for physical contact with others. We are predisposed to be touched. Without physical contact from others, people become *touch-starved*, *skin hungry,* or *touch deprived.*

Skin-to-skin contact is necessary for mental, emotional, and physical health. Research by Dr. Kory Floyd, an author and expert on affection deprivation, suggests that:

> "... people who feel more affection-deprived: are less happy; more lonely; more likely to experience depression and stress; and, in general, in worse health. They have less social support and lower relationship satisfaction. They experience more mood and anxiety disorders, and more secondary immune disorders (those that are acquired rather than inherited genetically). They are more likely to have *alexithymia*, a condition that impairs their ability to express and interpret emotion. Finally, they are more likely to have a preoccupied or fearful-avoidant attachment style; they're less likely to form secure attachments with others in their lives."

An implicit characteristic of love is **being desired**: being wanted, needed, and valued for the reciprocal love one gives; giving and receiving affection; and giving and receiving positive physical contact. When we are desired, we are objectively *attractive* to someone. This is something we know and can *feel*. The feeling enhances our notion of self, worth, and self-esteem.

Being *undesirable* can mean that one is not wanted, that they are unnecessary and insignificant. When a person is considered to be undesirable—which can be implied by being rejected, scorned, or not pursued for a loving relationship—the person's sense of self, worth, and value is diminished, potentially causing the person to behave **irrationally** in the hopes of becoming more desirable and worthy of affectionate love.

EXAMPLES OF DESIRABILITY-BASED IRRATIONALITY

"I'ma Cut That Bitch!"

The phrase "cut-a-bitch" has now become a part of our common vernacular. Various manifestations of the phrase, including "I'll cut a bitch," "I'll cut that bitch," and "I'ma cut that bitch," are used by people on the street, on television, by comedians—especially female comedians—and even in newspaper articles.

To *cut-a-bitch* can be defined differently, but, ultimately, the essence of the phrase signifies that someone is angry or confrontational, and is threatening another person with verbal or physical assault.

Question: If you overheard someone shouting, "I'ma cut that bitch!" what would you guess was happening? I posed this question to 103 mostly professional men and women at a conference. The response was not surprising to me: 76 of the 103 respondents (74%) said the situation was likely one where a man had cheated on a woman, and the cheated on woman was taking out her anger on the other woman. This survey result was unsurprising because the context the respondents assumed is the same context in which I primarily hear the phrase used. What was surprising, however, was that no one said the reverse, that a man was seeking vengeance against another man with whom his partner had cheated.

Data from the 2016 General Social Survey (GSS) on infidelity (i.e., cheating) found that *20% of men and 13% of women reported that they've had sex with someone other than their spouse while married. This may underestimate infidelity, however.* Some findings, like those presented in the *Journal of Marriage and Divorce*, conclude that 70% of married Americans cheat at least once in their marriage. It is more likely that one would hear a woman responding to a man's infidelity since, as both studies show, men cheat more often.

Several years ago, while visiting a relative in Philadelphia, our conversation was interrupted by shouts of, "Let me go! I'ma cut that bitch!" Watching the goings on, we learned that Woman A's boyfriend had been having an affair with Woman B, who happened to be a friend of Woman A. The two women would have certainly come to blows if not for the cheating man standing between them, separating the women.

I began to think about a question that would always arise whenever I saw a similar situation: Woman A gets cheated on by a man, so Woman A decides to take out her anger on the woman with whom the man had an affair, Woman B. Why is Woman A attacking Woman B, when it was the *man* who decided to disrespect his relationship by sleeping with Woman B? After all, I am sure that Woman B didn't assault the man or force him at gunpoint to have sex with her. The man had to be a willing participant at least, and the final decision maker at worst. In this instance, the *guilty party* is the one who has the final say as to whether or not an affair will be initiated. And, if I were a betting man, based on statistics, I would bet my house that the man approved the affair, making *him* the guilty party. Woman B? In terms of who's going to get "cut," she would be the wrongly-targeted person.

I have always believed it to be irrational that Woman A (or even a man in the same situation) would attack Woman B, when the blame more than likely sits at the feet of the man. Why not attack the *man* with equal or greater vengeance? While it may be against the law to "cut" either one of them, the person who is ultimately *accountable* for the infraction is the man, and, as such, he should be held to account. This would be rational. Blaming Woman B, as the person *accountable*, is irrational. An analysis of the situation could look like this:

1. Man and Woman A are in a loving relationship

2. Man meets Woman B

3. Man becomes intimate with Woman B

4. It is unlikely that Woman B *forced* the man to sleep with her, so it is reasonable to assume that Man acted of his own volition and made the conscious decision to disrespect his relationship with Woman A.

5. Upon learning of the affair, Woman A, understandably, is angry with Man.

6. However, the bulk of Woman A's wrath is directed toward Woman B, who she sees as the *real* culprit, the reason why Man cheated. To blame Woman B and want to "cut" or do harm to her while giving Man a slap on the wrist is, in my opinion, irrational.

**The person who is ultimately *accountable* for the infraction is the man, and, as such, he should be held to *account*.
This would be rational.**

Logically, the catalyst for the affair and its resulting damage to the relationship between Woman A and Man, can be identified as follows:

- If Man says "Yes" to the affair the affair will happen

- If Man says "No" to the affair, the affair will not happen

- If Woman B says "Yes" to the affair and Man says "No," the affair will not happen

- Therefore, Man is the approver and *guilty party,* because, without his approval, the affair would not happen. As such, he should—rationally—be the focal target of Woman A's scorn, not Woman B.

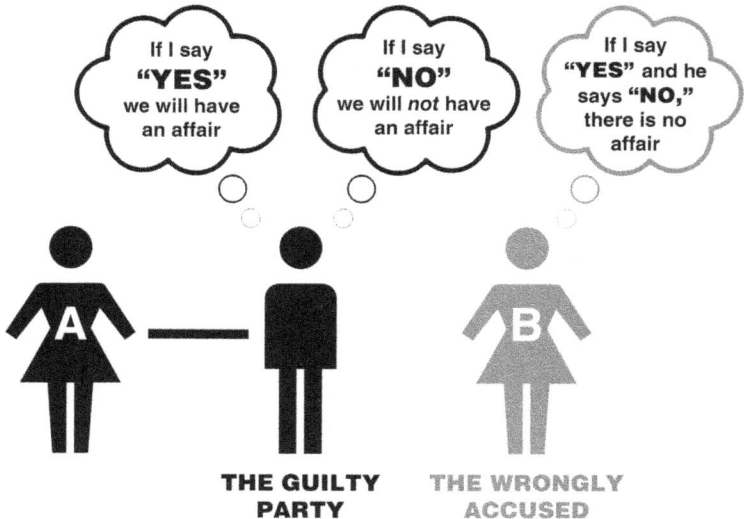

194

If my proposition is reasonable, then why does Woman A want to "cut"—literally, in far too many cases—Woman B? I believe the answer is because Woman A's feelings of desirability in general, and significance to Man specifically, have been negatively impacted. If she is no longer desirable to Man—as she could take away from his actions—then she could believe she is *undesirable* in general. To reiterate, being undesirable means that one is not wanted, and that they are seen as unnecessary and insignificant. When a person is considered to be undesirable—which can be implied by being rejected, scorned by an affair, or denied a loving relationship—the person's sense of self, worth, and value become diminished, potentially causing the person to behave irrationally in hopes of becoming more desirable and worthy of affectionate love. And how is irrational behavior manifest in this situation of Man cheating? By Woman A wanting to remove or dissuade Woman B from involvement in Woman A's life with Man—by "cutting that bitch."

It is reasonable to conclude that Woman A believes that, if Woman B was no longer in the picture, then the object (Woman B) that distracted Man from giving his love to Woman A would be gone, and Woman A would no longer only receive *half* of Man's love; she would get all of his love. This would redirect Man's focus back to Woman A, and restore not only their one-on-one loving relationship, but also Woman A's feelings of attractiveness, necessity, worth, and positive self-esteem.

You may be thinking that such reasoning by Woman A is misguided because **the man and the reason for his infidelity** is the issue that needs to be "resolved." While removing Woman B from Man's life might make Woman A feel good, it is unlikely to solve the problem of Man's straying. It's like brewing coffee.

The necessary components for brewing coffee are coffee, water, and a vehicle for passing the water through the coffee grounds, such as a filter. Suppose that one day Fred went to a friend's house where he enjoyed the most delicious cup of coffee he'd had in years. He followed his friend's process for making that delicious coffee: Fred's friend ground the coffee beans and measured the amount of water and coffee used. He then combined the two in his French press coffee maker, and, four minutes later, he'd made great coffee.

Eager to make delicious coffee for himself at home, Fred followed his friend's process precisely. He went to the local supermarket and purchased a bag of ground coffee, he purchased a measuring cup to measure the amount of coffee and water to use, and he headed home to make the coffee. He measured the proper amounts of water and coffee, as recommended by his friend. He doesn't own a French press coffee maker, so he used his trusty Mr. Coffee Coffee Maker. After the coffee finished brewing, Fred tasted it and *hated* it! The coffee was nowhere near as good as his friend's. He thought: "Maybe it's the coffee maker."

So, hoping to replicate his friend's coffee, Fred went out and purchased a French press, just like his friend's. He repeated the coffee-making process, this time using the French press, and got the same result: terrible coffee. Fred then thought the issue might be the *tap water* he used and *not* the coffee maker. So, he went out and purchased bottles of spring water, filtered water, electrolyte water, purified water, distilled/deionized water, and alkaline water. He made coffee using each type of water and got the same result: awful coffee.

Fred was stumped. He had tried everything he could think of—he purchased a new bag of ground coffee from the market, he tried several types of water, he purchased the French press. However, he could never recreate the taste of the coffee he had at his friend's house. So, he called his friend for advice. Fred described everything he'd done to make good coffee, but nothing worked. The friend said, "I know what the problem is. It is not the water or the coffee maker. It's the *coffee*."

The friend explained that after coffee beans are ground, they only remain at peak freshness for about two days. After that, freshness and taste diminish dramatically for another couple of days before the pre-ground coffee becomes stale and tastes awful. Fred finally realized that, no matter what he replaced, until he addressed the major contributor to good coffee—freshly roasted coffee beans, ground at the time of brewing—he would never resolve the issue.

COFFEE   WATER   MAKER   CUP

Woman A can *cut a bitch* and remove the tap water and the Mr. Coffee Coffee Maker (metaphors for Woman B) from Man's life, but until the coffee issue is resolved (a metaphor for Man and his reasons for cheating), Woman A will continue to have "bad coffee." When Woman A and Man decide to make the extra effort to buy and grind fresh coffee beans (metaphors for couples counseling, workshops, and a healthy dose of forgiveness), she and Man can address the real issue and make better coffee.

Look at me; I'm invisible!

The behavior I describe here can be characterized as an example of irrational behavior related to any of the five domains of significance. I include it here because I believe this type of behavior strongly relates to the need to feel **desired** as a means to strengthen self-worth and self-esteem.

To all of the prolific TikTok, Instagram, Facebook, and Snapchat photo and video clip uploaders, I have a simple message: people find you less interesting than you think you are. There are one billion TikTok users worldwide, but, according to *Statista*, less than one percent of users (0.6 percent, to be exact) have 500,000 or more subscribers. Sure. I get it: We all have some degree of a desire to be wanted, praised, admired, liked, and to feel important. And apps like these offer a platform for us to be seen and, hopefully ... wanted, praised, admired, liked, and deemed important. But some people have taken the desire (or need) to feel significant to new levels of attention-seeking behavior. Have you heard about the trips to Dubai taken by so-called "Instagram models" or the lengths men go to be dubbed an "alpha male"? Bizarre and irrational.

It is not only social media models and wannabe alpha males who behave irrationally in search of desirability. Legitimate, traditional media *supermodels*—"real" models, in the conventional sense—who seem to have it all: attractiveness, financial wealth, fame, notoriety, and a lifestyle of the rich and famous, have insecurities that compel *them* to act irrationally, though not necessarily to the degree of insanity.

During the late 1980s and into the '90s, Czechoslovak-born Swedish–American model Paulina Porizkova was the definition of a supermodel: She appeared on the covers of iconic magazines, including *Vogue*, *Elle*, *Harper's Bazaar*, *Cosmopolitan*, and *Sports Illustrated's* swimsuit issue to name just a few. In 1988, she signed a $6,000,000 contract with Estée Lauder, the most lucrative contract at the time. She was the highest-paid model in the industry, a legitimate "supermodel."

In a recent interview with The Times, the 56-year-old Porizkova said that she is "now completely invisible." She described how she once walked into a party and tried "to flirt with guys and they will just walk away from me mid-sentence to pursue someone 20 years younger. I'm very single, I'm dressed up, I've made an effort — nothing." She went on to say that her invisibility made her feel "really terrible about myself."

This is an example of Porizkova **tying her sense of self to her desirability**; she feels "terrible" about herself because she is now, in her opinion, invisible, which can be construed as undesirable. To become "visible," Porizkova began posting photos of herself in bikinis and nude. Is it rational for a woman to believe it is necessary to pose nude in photos and post them on social media just to become "visible," noticed, and desirable? I believe it is irrational, especially in light of Porizkova's statement in the interview in which she said women who have cosmetic procedures performed are: "actually servicing exactly what you're trying to oppose." In light of Porizkova's nude photos, that statement seems hypocritical.

Taking and posting sexy and nude photos of herself to compete on the same visibility-scale as 30-year-olds feeds into the sexist narrative that, as women get older, they feel the need to display their sexuality to feel desirable again.

V. PREEMINENCE

"Powerful people cannot afford to educate the people that they oppress, because once you are truly educated, you will not ask for power. You will take it."

–John Henrik Clarke

Preeminence is the quality of being more important or better than others. It relates to superiority. Through the belief of being better and more superior than others, one derives feelings of power, dominance, and a sense of entitlement, all of which preeminent people and those with what I refer to as *preeminence syndrome,* feel the need to exercise.

Preeminence Syndrome

Preeminence Syndrome (PeS) is a term I coined to describe a related set of behaviors exhibited by people with an inherent desire to reveal or demonstrate their actual or self-perceived **power, wealth, importance, or dominance** (PWID). One purpose of PeS-related behavior is to educate and make those unfamiliar with the perpetrator's *actual* PWID aware that s/he is ostensibly powerful, wealthy, important, or dominant. For instance, a preeminent person with PeS might behave in a manner that demonstrates their financial wealth and their V.I.P. status simultaneously. By doing so, they strengthen and enhance their notion of self, self-worth, and significance.

Another purpose for PeS-related behavior is to reinforce one's inner-belief that s/he is preeminent in some regard, whether or not the person has actually established a true measure of preeminence as manifest by relative power, financial wealth, importance, or dominance. This category of people is not actually determined to *be* preeminent based on *their* PWID relative to others who have achieved preeminence in the opinion of the majority, but hope to convince *themselves* that they are preeminent. This is a form of self-oriented or *self-serving lying*, telling lies to people not well-known to the perpetrator, with an aim of benefiting the preeminence-seeker.

In this sense, the preeminence-seeker is hoping that achieving actual preeminence becomes a self-fulfilling prophecy. By pretending to be preeminent and engaging in PeS- related behavior, the perpetrator hopes to convince enough people to think they are powerful, wealthy, important, or dominant, so that, when the people provide the perpetrator with enough positive, affirming reinforcement, the perpetrator will start to believe and internalize their feedback, ultimately convincing the perpetrator that s/he is legitimately preeminent.

My proposition here begs the question: How is it known or agreed upon that a person has achieved actual or "legitimate" preeminence? The short answer is *evidentiary proof.* How do we know Amazon CEO Jeff Bezos possesses PWID and is preeminent in his field? We can easily find examples of this. The same holds true for Berkshire Hathaway CEO Warren Buffett, former German Chancellor Angela Merkel, chess Grandmaster Magnus Carlsen, U.S. Congressman James Clyburn, attorney Alberto Gonzales, 17-year-old activists Xiuhtezcatl Roske-Martinez and Thandiwe Abdullah, and even Yulan Adonay Archaga Carias, the leader of the vicious Mara Salvatrucha (MS-13) gang.

There is a scene in the 1996 biopic *Basquiat,* about the life of Jean-Michel Basquiat—a young New York City artist and Andy Warhol associate who rose to success during the 1980s—where the titular character, after having achieved wealth and notoriety, met his former girlfriend in a swanky, high-end restaurant to talk.

Basquiat, who was African-American coiffed with dreadlocks, arrived at the restaurant looking like a homeless junkie. His face was carved with the telltale signs of drug use. A group of white men in suits was seated at a nearby table. Noticing Basquiat, they began pointing and laughing at the artist, thinking that he didn't belong in the same restaurant as them and that he certainly couldn't afford it. Noticing the men belittling him, Basquiat told the server to pay for the men's entire meal, on him, without the men knowing about it. Finding this peculiar, his friend asked why he would pay for the meals of men who obviously thought he was beneath them. Basquiat replied, "I mean, what year is this?"

Basquiat understood that there was no value in confronting the ignorant snobs, and the simple gesture of paying for all of their expensive meals would show the men that their perception of him was wrong: he did have the financial means to afford the restaurant, and they were not superior to him. The fact was, at the time, Basquiat was far wealthier than the men.

This movie scene exemplifies **PeS-related behavior** where the factually-preeminent person (Basquiat) demonstrated his wealth (by paying for the meals) and importance (by entering the restaurant looking like a homeless man and still being fawned over by the staff who knew who he was) to reveal to the unknowing snobbish white men that he was a person of preeminence. I believe that Basquiat's behavior was irrational. He should not have felt the need to behave this way just to prove his preeminence and worth to others, while simultaneously defending his notion of self and self-enhancement.

This example also reinforces the idea that factually-preeminent people have insecurities and are motivated by them to engage in irrational behavior. Whether relationship, body image, work, social, or other insecurities, everyone has them, even the most powerful people in the world, including American presidents.

In most cases, it is our insecurities that motivate us to behave irrationally, regardless of our condition, status, or standing. One of the laziest manifestations of one's insecurity is believing that the person's standing or feelings of self-worth will increase or improve by virtue of the prestige of a "competitor" or someone else decreasing. Experiencing self-satisfaction from the misfortunes of others is referred to as **Schadenfreude**, a German word loosely meaning *joy from damage or harm to others*. Schadenfreude makes insecure people feel better about themselves. It makes them feel more on-par or even superior to the person experiencing difficulties.

Desirability and prestige are the two domains of significance most obviously affected by Schadenfreude: "When that beautiful model got dumped and embarrassed on national television, it made me feel better about myself because their humiliation demonstrates that s/he is no more desirable than me." However, it also applies to the preeminence domain, whereby "That sales representative—who is said to be the best in the company—just lost his biggest account and will not make quota this year! I *will* make my quota, so he is not a superior sales representative to me after all. Damn, that feels good!"

This thinking is irrational because it took the "superior" sales rep's failure for the insecure sales rep to feel better about himself as a seller, even though this sales rep will achieve his own sales goal this year. Achieving a sales objective is a major accomplishment for any sales representative, and should itself strengthen the rep's worth, self-esteem, and value. So, if this insecure sales rep needs the other rep to fail to feel more worthy and valuable in the company, it is a sign of an **intrinsic inferiority** perception, forcing the insecure rep to behave irrationally.

EXAMPLES OF PREEMINENCE-BASED IRRATIONALITY

Racism: As a Threat to Preeminence

At its core, racism is an ideology of racial domination, power, and oppression of a particular racial group, such as African-Americans. Historian and *New York Times* best-selling author Dr. Ibram X. Kendi proposed that: "A racist idea is any idea that suggests one racial group is inferior to or superior to another racial group in any way. Racist ideas argue that the inferiorities and superiorities of racial groups explain racial inequities in society."

Racism is about one group—a group **with impactful power**—determining that their race is better than that of another race. This ideology is exemplified by white supremacy, which is the belief that white people, who have impactful power, are superior to others solely because of their race. The idea that whites were superior to African-Americans stemmed from so-called "scientific judgments" of the 1890s—an attempted rationalization that light-skinned people had greater intelligence and a higher degree of civilization than darker-skinned people, and were therefore superior.

As distinguished historian Richard D. Brown wrote in the article *White Supremacy and Privilege: Legacies of Slavery*: "The contradiction between slavery, the absolute embodiment of hereditary privilege, and its obverse, hereditary disadvantage, is absolute." Anglo-American slavery embedded the idea of **negrophobia**, a dislike of African-Americans by whites, in society. Their rationale, according to Brown was that: "Heathens, bought and sold like beasts, could not be the equals of free Englishmen and Americans ..."

There is a common set of recurring themes within this discussion of racism and white supremacy, namely advantage, dominance, superiority, privilege, hierarchy, the maintenance of oppression (wealth), and power. Any threat to these **unnatural advantages** can cause even otherwise rational people to behave irrationally.

There is a common set of recurring themes within this discussion of racism and white supremacy, namely: advantage, dominance, superiority, privilege, hierarchy, the maintenance of oppression (wealth), and power. Any threat to these *unnatural advantages* can cause even otherwise rational people to behave irrationally.

There are reasons why people have racist ideas. This includes insecurity (*My group is better than that group, so let's keep it that way by oppressing that "inferior" group*); easy scapegoating and blaming others for one's inadequacies (*I can't get a job because of "those" people*); negrophobia, and even fear (*Those "lesser" people are gaining in preeminence; I can't let them become superior to me. That would mean that I am beneath the low status I ascribe to them, and my unnatural advantages would disappear*).

During the period of enslavement, whites in many colonies instituted laws forbidding enslaved people from learning to read or write. It was also a crime for anyone to teach them how to read or write. As spelled out in The South Carolina Act of 1740:

> "Whereas, the having slaves taught to write, or suffering them to be employed in writing, may be attended with great inconveniences; Be it enacted, that all and every person and persons whatsoever, who shall hereafter teach or cause any slave or slaves to be taught to write, or shall use or employ any slave as a scribe, in any manner of writing whatsoever, hereafter taught to write, every such person or persons shall, for every such offense, forfeit the sum of one hundred pounds, current money."

They feared that educating Black people would lead to Black independence (no longer relying on masters), which would threaten the entire system of slavery itself. What would follow, they believed, was not only a decrease in wealth but also a **loss of power.** The legacy of white supremacy and inherent unnatural advantage is exemplified through racism, which some consider a **mental illness**. Throughout history, defending advantages has led people to not only behave irrationally but also pathologically. In their paper *Pathological Racism, Chronic Racism & Targeted Universalism*, law professors Charles and Fuentes-Rohwer refer to such racism-based behavior as examples of "pathological racism," because of its particular virulence.

I believe that every act of racism is directed toward defending some aspect of the *preeminence* domain of significance: Power, wealth, importance, or dominance (PWID).

- **Power and wealth:** Throughout history, as racial minorities gained "freedom," became educated, amassed property and wealth, gained equal rights under the law, won election to public office, ascended to the tops of organizations, and achieved the highest levels of fame and significance that one could achieve, racists have viewed such progress as a threat to their preeminence.

  Fundamentally, "wealth" is the value of all marketable assets a person or family owns, minus any debts. "Power" is the ability or wherewithal to realize one's ambitions or goals, even in the face of opposition. In his book "Power: A Radical View," author Steven Lukes describes the nature of power as a utility relationship between "A" and "B," in which A and B can be a person or a group. "A exercises power over B when A affects B in a manner contrary to B's interests." A relationship exists between wealth and power. Wealth is a resource that can be used for power, and power can lead to wealth. Those who have the most wealth are the most powerful.

So, how could white colonists—in the hopes of maintaining their preeminence—pass a racist law in 1740 that prohibited slaves from learning or being taught? It's simple: the colonists were members of a society with common attitudes about white supremacy. They possessed all the wealth and held all the power to do so.

- **Importance:** Importance is the state of being of great value. While it is often used synonymously with the word "significance," I propose that, though they are similar, there is a distinction, which can be explained using the aforementioned "island question." If you were stranded on an unknown island hoping to survive as long as possible, a weapon would be *important*—given the unknowns—but water would be *necessary*. So, while a weapon might be important and affect your survival and well-being, water is *necessary* for your survival. Unless something is deemed necessary, it cannot be declared significant.

Preeminent people are, within specific contexts, considered to be important. Therefore, importance is a condition of preeminence. However, they lose their perceived and factual preeminence when they become unimportant.

American former film producer and convicted sex offender Harvey Weinstein was, at one point, legitimately preeminent. He and his brother Bob co-founded Miramax, a highly successful film and entertainment company. Before his arrest in May of 2018, Weinstein was, by all accounts, the most powerful man in Hollywood, a distinction formally confirmed when, in 2012, TIME named him "The Most Powerful Man in Hollywood." Weinstein had legitimate PWID.

Today, as he sits in the Twin Towers Correctional Facility in Los Angeles awaiting trial, he is not only disgraced but also completely unimportant and powerless. For this reason, he is no longer a dominant figure and undoubtedly not preeminent.

Importance brings about wealth, and wealth leads to power. Power makes racist legislation, like The South Carolina Act of 1740, possible. Oppressing people by keeping them poor and illiterate preserved white colonists' perceived superiority and dominance over enslaved Africans.

- **Dominance:** Dominance is an expected outcome of relationships between people who compete for resources that satisfy fundamental human needs. When people compete for the same resource—food, partners, money, land, opportunity, etc.—each individual will behave in a way that benefits themselves over the other person, ultimately leading to conflict. There are lots of ways for individuals to resolve conflict. Some approaches for gaining agreement or compromise are easy (e.g., deference to age), and others are not, such as fighting. Over time, the parties will naturally establish a relationship of circumstantial dominance over each other, through which the dominant person gets their way, and the subordinate person does not. Dominance is about achieving power; the ability to set the terms under which other groups and classes operate. It relates to gaining and sustaining an advantage and superiority.

  If insecure white supremacists lost their unnatural advantage of dominance—legal or otherwise—over formerly enslaved "Heathens, bought and sold like beasts," who, "could not be the equals of free Englishmen and Americans," their own sense of worth would be diminished. Their actual or perceived preeminence would weaken, giving rise to feelings of insignificance—assuming the unnatural advantage of self-perceived superiority was the cornerstone of a racist's worth.

"Kayne HAS to STOP This"

During a recent YouTube podcast entitled, "Kayne HAS to STOP This," clinical psychologist Dr. Umar Johnson responded to a caller's question asking what has to be done to get African-Americans to curb their materialism. Johnson replied:

> "If you study the economic behavior of Black people since emancipation, you will see that our spending behavior is not motivated by needs or desires, they are motivated by emotions.
>
> Black people spend ... **to outdo other Black people**. Everything we buy is based on status: 'I want to outdo other Black people, and I want to feel better about my reality.' ... If you your Timberlands [boots] get one *scratch*, you're gonna get another pair of Timberlands. What's wrong with that scratch on your Timberlands? You feel that it lessens your **value**. Slavery *took* our **self-worth**, so now we are replacing it, ironically, with white-man-made materials."

Irrational behavior in the hopes of achieving status and preeminence ("I'm better than you") is not solely the domain of factually-preeminent people. People with less wealth than the truly "wealthy"—and certainly those with little-to-no financial resources—will try to elevate themselves within their community, even if their behavior is irrational.

Say You're Sorry!

We've been taught since we could talk that it is right and proper to apologize when we have erred. By doing so, we were taught, we would not only patch things up with the aggrieved party, but it would also make us feel better about ourselves. An apology shows humility, which makes us better people.

I believe, however, that asking for or demanding an apology from someone, or even expecting one from a perpetrator, demonstrates superiority. Apologizing and saying, "I'm sorry," is very hard for people to do, and can detract from one's sense of self. To the apology-seeking receiver, an apology is about the power dynamic between the two parties involved; making someone—or having someone else make them—give you an apology demonstrates your superiority. It is as if the apology-seeker was saying: "Come to me with humility and share with me your shame!"

Getting an apology does help mend relationships, if for no other reason than the dominance-seeking person will "forgive" (a God-like **power gesture**) the offender and "allow" (also a demonstration of power) the relationship to proceed on good footing.

Receiving an apology is a gesture to show that the bad actor acknowledges the effect of their behavior, absolves the aggrieved of any fault, wants to undo any harm, and wants to imply that the offender will be a better person going forward. It shows they want to mend any harm and restore trust in the relationship. For these reasons, receiving an apology is beneficial for both parties. However, *needing*, demanding, or desperately wanting an apology from another person is irrational. Apologies make the needy aggrieved person feel good for the aforementioned reasons of power, superiority, and preeminence, which I contend is irrational.

The ultimate value of one's contrition is that the apology-worthy event serves as a catalyst for personal growth by the offender and for strengthening the relationship. One's demonstration of growth and contrition will have a greater impact on a relationship than one's words or a spoken apology. Which is more desirable: (A) an offender offering the sincerest of heartfelt apologies but not changing their behavior or demonstrating real contrition or growth; or (B) an offender who didn't apologize for an offense, but changed their behavior and demonstrated contrition and growth through their *actions*, ultimately leading to a strengthened relationship of trust?

If the desired outcome from making a mistake is realizing the mistake, learning from it, improving by changing behavior, and becoming a better person, family member, friend, and citizen, then that outcome is only achieved through *actions*, not words. Is it really necessary to demand that a person who is undoubtedly remorseful and ashamed of their apology-worthy behavior needs to verbalize their contrition through an apology? I want to reiterate that I believe apologies are good and have value. However, it is the *needing* and *demanding* of an apology from a person who has wronged you that I believe is irrational.

If the desired outcome from making a mistake is realizing the mistake, learning from it, improving by changing behavior, and becoming a better person, family member, friend, and citizen, then that outcome is only achieved through actions, not words.

HUMILITY

Do you wish to rise? Begin by descending. You
plan a tower that will pierce the clouds? Lay
first the foundation of humility."

-SAINT AUGUSTINE-

*M*ahayana Buddhism, a major school of Buddhism practiced in China, Taiwan, Japan, and Korea, advocates **humility** as a moral principle. Buddhists believe that only through humility can one recognize their own destructive cravings, aversion or hatred, and ignorance. Until humility becomes a moral precept, insecurities—such as those that motivate people to behave irrationally—will prevent people from becoming liberated or experiencing the state of enlightenment, which comes when one transcends the destructiveness of self-aggrandizement or ego. Yet, humility is not an under-evaluation of one's self-worth or value. Dr. Chen Yu-His, Professor of Religious Studies at Fo Guang University in Taiwan, put it provocatively when he wrote: "The quintessence of humility is manifested in a practitioner's realization that he is nobody or nothing."

Acknowledgement Begets Humility

A more practical reading of *humility* is that, in its simplest form, it is freedom from arrogance, and, at its most complex, narcissism. I propose that the path toward humility—and ultimately, significance—begins with an acknowledgment that:

- You are not perfect, nor will you ever achieve a state of perfection, because **perfection** is a level of excellence that cannot be exceeded.

- You will make mistakes, lots of them, and some worse than others.

- You don't know everything; you cannot. So, you will be wrong about most things.

- You are not as appealing as you think you are, but that's okay. Appeal is not all about physical beauty (which is, by the way, subjective) or desirability.

- You're not as impressive as you think you are. Way back in 1800, Italian physicist Alessandro Volta created a steady flow of electrical charge, which was basically electricity as we know it today. Back in 1800! *That's* impressive.

- Not everyone likes you, nor will *everyone* ever like you. But that's okay.

- You have insecurities. Therefore, at some point ...

- **You will behave irrationally** in the pursuit, strengthening, or defense of domains of significance; it is a part of being human.

Humility, self-worth, value, and significance are not mutually-exclusive. People with a high sense of worth have the ability to make mistakes and learn from them. They don't place blame at the feet of others and they use failure as an opportunity for growth and development. An individual with a positive sense of self has the ability to accept his or her shortcomings, which is a form of self-acceptance: understanding one's personal strengths and limitations, acknowledging one's imperfections, and having the confidence that one can *make improvements* in their life.

All Improvement Requires Change (and So Does Significance)

All improvement requires change. Is there anything that can be improved without having to do something differently? No.

"Improvement" comes from learning. It is about making changes that will lead to a better place. But change is not easy. As humans, we are predisposed to the status quo for self-preservation. Yet, as humans, we have an unquenchable thirst for knowledge and exploration—catalysts for new discoveries and human progress. However, without change, there can be no improvement, no progress.

Change requires knowledge and the acknowledgement that **we are flawed** human beings. If, for example, a man wants to become a better husband, which would require him to be a better listener, the man must first learn (gain the knowledge) that his poor listening skills are hurting his marriage. Then, the man would have to acknowledge and *accept* that unpleasant reality (i.e., be humble), learn from it, and develop an improvement plan. While such an acknowledgement might bruise his ego and reduce his self-esteem ("What? I am not a perfect *listener*?"), ultimately, becoming a better listener will lead to becoming a better husband.

The man will change his behavior when he determines that a change is worthwhile. He will start by weighing, in a systematic way, the pluses and minuses of making a change based on how he believes the change will help him become a better husband. He may reason that achieving such an outcome could positively affect his notion of self ("I am imperfect, but I am willing to be better"), strengthen his self-esteem, ("I have become a good listener!"), and increase his sense of value and perception of significance ("I am a better husband").

Oftentimes, however, knowledge of our imperfections draws out uncomfortable feelings and emotions, including embarrassment, disappointment, sadness, personal pain, rejection, or other insecurities. The truth is that these unpleasant feelings and emotions are normal, and to not experience them is to be either a zombie or a psychopath. We learn from these feelings and emotions; experiencing them teaches us to not only cope with them, but also how to mitigate or avoid them. To appreciate happiness, we must know what it is to be unhappy. To avoid pain, we must experience and appreciate pain. We experience pain for a reason: pain is a teacher. It helps us change behaviors to thrive. We experience disappointment for a reason: it helps us change the way we do things, make improvements, and evolve as human beings. We experience discomfort for a reason: it is our body's way of telling us that something needs to be altered or fixed for us to improve and feel better. The common thread running through all of our undesirable feelings, thoughts, and emotions, such as fear, pain, discomfort, sadness, disappointment, loneliness, rejection, and insecurity, is the need for *change* to improve the underlying situations that rouse these feelings, thoughts, and emotions. Improvement requires change, and to make change possible, you must confront your negative feelings, thoughts, and emotions. Our confrontation begins with humility: **I am not perfect.**

Humility, self-worth, value, and significance are not mutually exclusive. People with a high sense of worth have the ability to make mistakes and learn from them. They don't place blame at the feet of others and they use failure as an opportunity for growth and development.

How do we become less insecure across the domains of significance? I don't believe that anyone has the complete answer, including me. Although I have some thoughts on the matter beyond practicing humility, my ideas are not fully formed. My intention is not to be prescriptive about conquering domains of significance. Instead, it is to identify what I propose is the cause for our everyday irrational behaviors—namely, **the pursuit of significance**—and to provide an understanding of the domains of significance that impact our degree of significance.

So, it is my postulate that **all human beings seek to achieve, strengthen, or defend the domains of significance for their impact in significance; and in doing so, we often behave irrationally.**

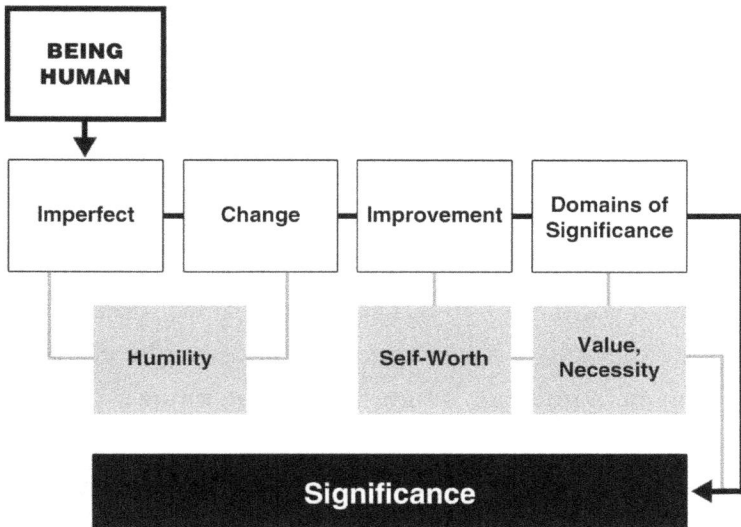

"I Am Wrong"

"We're trying to prove ourselves wrong as quickly as possible, because only in that way can we find progress."

- Richard Feynman,
  theoretical physicist and Nobel Prize recipient

Humility requires an acknowledgement that we are not perfect. Instead, we are fallible and will make mistakes. One of the most difficult things to do when we have made a mistake is to be humble and admit the mistake. This requires acknowledging that we've erred, which creates an internal contradiction: "I am the most attractive, most popular, most desirable person in the school." One month later: "No one has asked me to the prom, and the people I've asked—even the *losers*—all said 'no'."

As human beings, our intrinsic notion of self is attached to our ideas, opinions, beliefs, and behaviors, all of which contribute to our **identity**—our notion of self. When the self is threatened by the thought of being wrong or admitting wrongdoing, our natural instinct to defend our *self* kicks in, and we defend against being wrong by fighting to prove we were right. Such internal battles—"The evidence suggests I am wrong, but I'm going to prove that I am right no matter what"—create contradictory thoughts: "I'm attractive, popular, and desirable," and "No one will go to the prom with me. Maybe I'm not so attractive, popular, or desirable after all." Psychologists refer to this internal struggle as **cognitive dissonance**.

"Cognitive dissonance" occurs when we have conflicting or inconsistent thoughts, beliefs, or behaviors, making us uncomfortable or mentally stressed. The dissonance (disharmony between thoughts or behaviors) threatens our notion of self, leading us to try to reduce or eliminate the discomfort.

At this point, the person has a choice to make. They can attempt to defend themselves against being wrong by using a "defense mechanism." For example, "I didn't want to go to prom with those people *anyway*. They are not on my level." Alternatively, they could acknowledge that their thoughts, opinions, or behaviors were wrong: "Hmm. Maybe I'm not as likeable or friendly as I thought I was. How can I be better?" The latter, however, is easier said than done.

Humility requires an acknowledgement that we are not perfect. Instead, we are fallible and will make mistakes.

True to the theme of this book, I once had an experience with another author which demonstrated how otherwise rational people behave irrationally when defending domains of significance, such as those related to making mistakes and being perceived as or proven to be wrong.

Once, on a red-eye flight from Los Angeles to Philadelphia, I was sitting next to a young man who had written his first book manuscript. As we struck up a conversation, he learned that I had written a few books and started asking for my advice. He planned to self-publish the book and was handling all aspects of the process herself, including hiring an editor.

About 45 minutes into the flight, he asked if I would take a look at her manuscript—which was printed on paper—and offer some suggestions. As I got to the halfway point of the third page, I told him, "If you'd like, I can do some markups of any major issues I see." He agreed. Mind you, when it comes to writing, I am no Leo Tolstoy or even the excellent Percival Everett; not even in the same stratosphere. However, since the man's manuscript looked like my then 8th-grade son had written it, I figured I could handle that.

By the time I had finished marking up the first chapter—nearly *two hours later*—I turned to the man and suggested he work with an editor (I gave him a few recommendations) and explained my reason for the recommendation. "There's a *lot* that needs to be fixed. Maybe a content editor can help you re-craft it." Internally, I thought, "He should probably just start over from scratch; it'll be faster." The manuscript was unreadable, confusing, had inconsistent story lines, and was grammatically in need of a lifeline, to name just a few of the issues. It was shockingly bad. I remember thinking, "My 8th-grade son would actually write a better manuscript, and he *hates* school and *loathes* writing book reports."

Months later, I wondered what had happened to the author and his book, so I looked it up on Amazon.com, and there it was! I ordered a copy, and, when it arrived, I ripped open the packaging and dove right in. I read the first paragraph. It was the same as the problematic manuscript I'd already read. I completed the first chapter; the same thing. I was shocked! He hadn't changed *anything*!

Curious about what happened since the plane ride, I dug out his business card and sent him an email, saying I had bought his book. He gave me a call:

"Hi, Tab! This is 'Author.' I'm so glad you bought my book. Thank you!"

After exchanging pleasantries, I asked, "As I read the book, I noticed it was exactly the same as the manuscript you showed me. Did you use an editor? Just curious."

"Yes," he replied, to my surprise. "I used a woman named 'Editor' who is a co-worker of a friend of mine at the local college. 'Editor' was great! She said that I was a very good writer, and that there were not many edits needed." I was baffled.

"Did you check out the editors I suggested?" Yes, he said, "But I didn't have a good rapport with either of them."

Still baffled, I reached out to the recommended editors and asked if "Author" had contacted them. Editor #1 said that she'd read the first chapter and declined to work on it; it simply needed too much work. Editors #2 and 3 each had offered to work with "Author," and each had the same experience. They both said they had reviewed his first chapter and basically had to rewrite it because it was so bad. They also said that, when they discussed their sample edits with "Author" by phone, "Author" was offended. According to the editors, "Author" said, "Well, I disagree. I think the chapter is good as it is. Maybe it needs a few punctuation fixes, but it does not need to be rewritten. In fact, I sent it to another editor who said that it was very good, so that's who I am going to use."

After speaking with my recommended editors, I looked at the book's reviews on Amazon.com; the average of the four reviews was 1.5 stars. The reviewers' comments were harsh, echoing my feedback to "Author" and the sentiments of my recommended editors.

"Author" was a textbook example of someone struggling with cognitive dissonance, who elected to protect his feelings and prove himself right ("'Editor' was great! She said that I was a very good writer, and that there were not many edits needed."), instead of acknowledging the need for changes that would improve the book. The result was that he released an embarrassing book that likely did more harm to his self-esteem than acknowledging the need for change would have. Today, "Author's" book is no longer available for sale on Amazon.com.

Acknowledging you are wrong is a **first step toward improvement**, personal growth, and development. It demonstrates that you value honesty, truth, and your pursuit of achieving significance more than you value your need to be right or infallible.

Acknowledging you are wrong is a first step toward improvement, personal growth, and development. It demonstrates that you value honesty, truth, and your pursuit of achieving significance more than you value your need to be right or infallible.

When one acknowledges that they are wrong, it opens the door to considerations for improvement. Since improvement requires change, the person would have to modify their behavior or chart a different course to achieve a different outcome. Changing behavior can elevate a person to new discoveries, leading to happiness and fulfillment. When one becomes willing to be wrong, in the pursuit of truth, they grow to understand that being wrong and making a mistake is not tragic. It is, instead, an opportunity to become better, thereby increasing one's notion of self and all of the benefits that brings. Consider the two scenarios below:

Scenario 1: You Are an Infallible 16-Year-Old

Imagine being 16 years old, that dangerous age where you think you know everything, but you actually know very little. Now imagine that you had to live with the consequences of every decision you make and every action you take from age 16 until today—assuming you are older than 16 now. Put differently, you must live with every decision you make or action you take as a 16-year-old. No do-overs, no "oops," no trial-and-error, no correcting your mistakes, nothing. Why? Because you have convinced yourself that you are infallible, you don't make mistakes, and you are never wrong about anything. In this case, you are either a **sophomaniac** (believing the delusion that you have superior intelligence), a narcissist, or a fool.

Think of the negative consequences of believing you are infallible and, because of this delusion, never changing your actions, behavior, thoughts, opinions, or beliefs.

- If, for example, you believed that *your* opinion of how things work superseded that which your teachers were trying to teach you or the content of the books you read, would you graduate high school?

- Could you graduate college—assuming you saw a need to go to college? After all, you already believe you know everything.

- Could you survive into adulthood?

- Could you maintain a healthy relationship?

- Could you raise a child causing the least amount of damage possible?

- Could you hold down a job?

- If arrested and paroled, would you continue the behavior for which you had been arrested in the first place, just because you thought you were right and your behavior was just?

- Could you run a business?

- Would you ever find happiness and contentment?

- Would daily cognitive dissonance drive you mad?

The implications are truly frightening.

Scenario 2: You Are a 16-Year-Old Imperfect Human Being

Again, imagine that you are that same 16-year-old. In this scenario, however, you realize that people make mistakes and that no one is perfect, including you. Answer those same ten questions. Would you have more confidence that you would lead a happier, more fulfilling life as a fallible, imperfect 16-year-old than you would if you thought and behaved as the infallible 16-year-old thought and believed?

The lesson from this admittedly extreme scenario is that—history shows—life is better when you can accept being wrong about things, make mistakes, learn from your mistakes, and use the experience and knowledge to become better.

One of the most impactful yet underrealized reasons people find it difficult to self-improve is that we succumb to the dopamine-like good feelings we receive that result from our irrational behaviors directed toward defending our domains of significance. For example, if I feel insecure about my level of prestige as a professional athlete, I will buy a flashy $30,000 Rolex watch. By doing so, I am subliminally hoping that the watch will serve as a status symbol and create a (false) illusion to others that I am prestigious, which will counter-balance my insecurities born of my impoverished upbringing. If the illusion works and people begin to believe that I am prestigious, I hope that their belief will become a self-fulfilling prophecy.

This irrational approach to gaining prestige is counterproductive because if I rest on the belief that my Rolex watch has hypnotized people into ascribing prestige to me, I will not take the steps necessary to become prestigious truly. Ultimately, I will waste valuable time basking in the glow of false prestige when I could use that time to put in the necessary work to become genuinely prestigious.

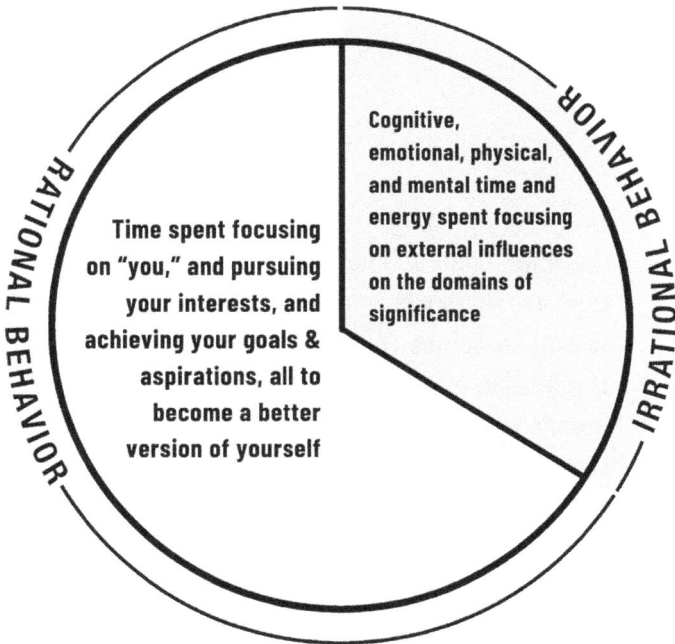

WHY DO WE EXIST? REVISITED

There will come a time when all of us are dead. All of us. There will come a time when there are no human beings remaining to remember that anyone ever existed or that our species ever did anything. ... Everything that we did and built and wrote and thought and discovered will be forgotten and all of this will have been for naught."

-JOHN GREEN-
AUTHOR, "THE FAULT IN OUR STARS"

REVISITING THE QUESTION: WHY DO WE EXIST?

What is our purpose on earth, our destination; why do we exist? There is no *definitive* answer to this existential question. So, since it can be rationally assumed that we have no other-directed purpose on earth, the next question is: What ultimate purpose should we aspire to achieve? Since there is also no universal, definitive answer to *that* question, then the only factual answer can be that, while we exist, we should maximize our capacity and pursue that which brings us **life satisfaction**. We should strive to be happy, but happy on our own terms, and to experience living a full, high-quality life that is meaningful—purpose-driven.

By its simplest definition, "fulfillment" is achieving something significant that one has set out to do, such as, entering into a loving union with a partner, raising a family, being active in the community, and experiencing regular happiness throughout the journey. Another example of fulfillment as a life destination or purpose is, for instance, the student who wants to become a healthcare professional, gaining inner peace, a sense of significance, and life satisfaction through providing medical services and public health education to underserved and vulnerable communities globally.

Fulfillment also demonstrates the successful culmination of one's potential. By this definition, basketball superstar LeBron James would not be fulfilled working as an attorney. From the time he was a child, his potential as a great basketball player was evident, and his dreams of playing basketball for a living aspirational. Anything short of reaching the National Basketball Association (NBA) as a player would have been considered a failure, for it was only by fulfilling his basketball potential and becoming the best player in the world that LeBron could achieve life satisfaction and fulfillment.

One might ask: "This definition of fulfillment as *achieving one's aspirations and maximizing their capacity and potential* implies that one cannot achieve personal fulfillment, satisfaction, and meaning in life by simply loving God through worship, as is written in the scriptures. Personally, I am fulfilled by worshipping God."

That is a fair question. I believe that life satisfaction comes when we define that which makes us happy on our own terms. So, if one finds happiness and fulfillment through worship then, to that person, reaching an afterlife is likely the achievement of their life's aspiration, leading to fulfillment. On this point of self-fulfillment, I believe there is wisdom in the perspective of author and moral philosopher Alan Gewirth, as he wrote in "Self-Fulfillment":

> " ... other ideals or norms have value only insofar as they serve, directly or indirectly, to further personal self-fulfillment. Morality, religion, aesthetics, and other realms of value may focus on actions and institutions, on artifacts, on nature with its living beings and environmental ecology, and on many other kinds of objects. But insofar as these are values for human beings, they come down finally to impacts on the development or fruition of the human self. It is how the human self experiences these objects or relates to them regarding its fulfillment that determines, in the final analysis, whether and how they are good or bad, right or wrong."

"Fulfillment" is achieving something significant that one has set out to do, such as, entering into a loving union with a partner, raising a family, being active in the community, and experiencing regular happiness throughout the journey.

SELF-DETERMINATION AND FULFILLMENT:
A PHILOSOPHICAL DEBATE

I am a steadfast believer in the value of one's self-interest. People acting in their self-interest (as opposed to *selfishly*, which holds, at its core, the quality of harm to self or others) is good for the person and, ultimately, good for society.

Self-determination is the idea that each individual has control over their choices and life, which plays an important role in an individual's health and well-being. The notion that people have the right to live their lives as they determine to be in their own self-interest is what relates self-interest and self-determination. If a person decides that the pursuit of their aspiration—however they determine it—is what will bring them inner peace and fulfillment, then, philosophically, they could argue that their life's pursuit toward fulfilling their self-determined aspiration is a good thing, because achieving it, would lead to fulfillment.

The flaw with this *anything-that-I-decide-to-do-is-good-because-it-will-be-in-pursuit-of-that-which-brings-me-happiness* belief is that some pursuits could be irrational.

For example, what if a person addicted to heroin decided that their life's pursuit—their aspiration—is to make enough money to buy enough heroin that they would *never* have to come down off of their high and become sick. The person might argue from the position of self-interest that, "It is in my self-interest to keep myself from becoming dope-sick." The person could also argue that nothing brings them more inner peace and fulfillment than ingesting the drug. While these arguments might seem compelling, in my opinion, they fail to meet the **threshold of rationality** which I believe is a condition for such societally-extreme positions to be considered good.

Rationality assumes that people are basically **mentally healthy and sane**, they exercise sound judgment, and use common sense when making decisions. It is debatable whether or not a heroin addict is acting rationally or, depending on how far gone they are, if they are still mentally healthy. According to The National Institute on Drug Abuse, drug addiction is a mental illness. It affects the addict's brain, disrupting their normal hierarchy of needs and making the procurement and use of their drug of choice their priority need. This weakens their ability to control impulses, *despite the negative consequences*, similar to the characteristics of other mental illnesses.

Given this condition of rationality, I do not believe that living as a full-time heroin addict can be one's life aspiration bringing fulfillment, because the decision to pursue such a course would not be made by a person of sound mind and body. I also believe that one cannot *logically* define their life's goal to be a heroin addict; addiction is not an end state goal for anyone, including even an addict. It would be the equivalent of saying, "When I smoke cigarettes, I feel relaxed, my nerves are calmed, my hands don't shake, and I can get things done. When I don't have cigarettes, I go through withdrawal and can neither function nor care for my children. Therefore, my life's goal is to never run out of cigarettes so that I can become a better parent."

An Answer

To reiterate, Aristotle believed that human beings have a *telos*, an inherent purpose, similar to the notion of a goal or true function in life. He believed that human beings are "rational animals" with the ability to reason and to act on reason. And, since human beings have the ability to reason, we should pursue our telos— our inherent purpose or that which we are best suited to do. Therefore, he argued, our function in life is to *realize our potential as rational beings.*

It is never irrational, injurious, inconsiderate, useless, foolhardy, wasteful, or unwelcomed to do something agreeably-good for yourself, your friends, your family, your community, or the planet. While we may never agree on our specific purpose, I believe this is something on which we can all agree: rational people being good is desired by all.

If we can all find that rare common ground and agree that being good, considerate, respectful, and honest to both ourselves and others is a noble way of living, then, I believe, this is something to which we can all aspire in our pursuit of leading a worthwhile, fulfilling life. This, I propose, is our only rational purpose in life: to have a positive impact and contribute to a better life for all.

So, if we can all find that rare common ground and agree that being good, considerate, respectful, and honest to both ourselves and others is a noble way of living, then, I believe, this is something to which we can all aspire in our pursuit of leading a worthwhile, fulfilling life. This, I propose, is **our only rational purpose in life: to have a positive impact on and contribute to a better life for all.**

To best position ourself to make an impact, we must first intrinsically feel good about ourselves. Our well-being is predicated upon the belief that we are worthy of love and caring; we are valuable members of our families and society; and we are purposeful in our pursuit of fulfillment. Our continued growth and development as human beings requires that we be humble and behave rationally. It is okay to be imperfect, flawed, and mistake-prone, for it is how we behave in the face of these and other threats to our sense of self and the domains of significance that our true significance is revealed.

●

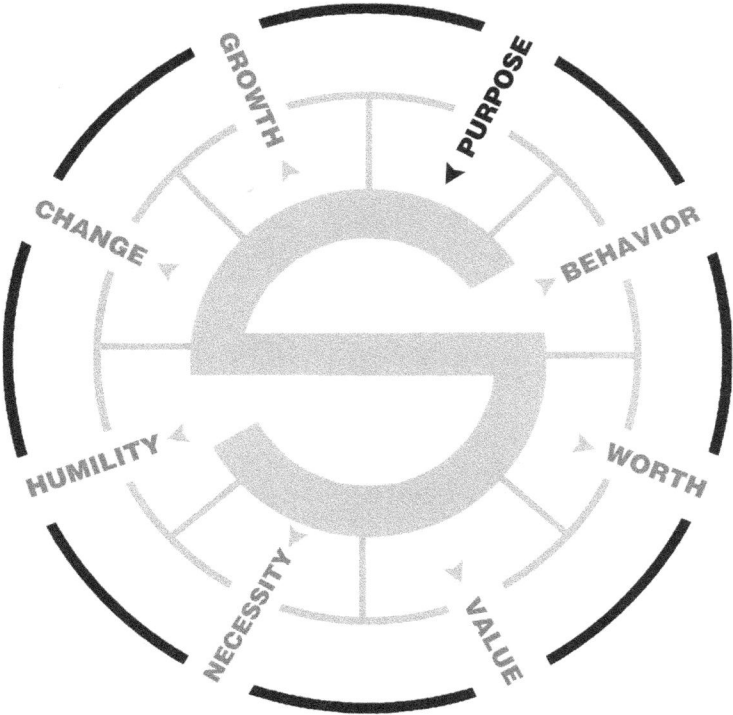

ABOUT THE AUTHOR

*T*ab Edwards is a best-selling author and globally-recognized thought-leader, critical thinker, and self-proclaimed rationalist. He works with organizations and individuals of all stripes on becoming "better" at their pursuits or aspirations. His principles have been adopted by people and organizations around the world, and his practices implemented globally.

Edwards is the co-founder and moderator of The Performance Laboratory No 33 ("The Lab #33"), an open think tank of thought-leaders, critical thinkers, and those who contribute to existing knowledge in their fields of expertise, working together to solve pressing problems. His expertise includes strategy and execution, and performance improvement at the individual and organizational levels.

He holds a bachelor's degree from The University of Pittsburgh, and a Master of Business Administration degree from The Pennsylvania State University.

VISIT TAB EDWARDS AT

WWW.TABEDWARDS.COM

WWW.TABEDWARDS.COM/SIGNIFICANCE

INFO@THELAB33.COM

NOTES

Leslie, John. "The Theory That the World Exists Because It Should." American Philosophical Quarterly, vol. 7, no. 4, 1970, pp. 286–298. JSTOR, www.jstor.org/stable/20009361. Accessed 19 July 2021.

Nelson, Michael, "Existence", *The Stanford Encyclopedia of Philosophy* (Summer 2020 Edition), Edward N. Zalta (ed.), URL = https://plato.stanford.edu/archives/sum2020/entries/existence/

Rana, Preetika. "How a Chinese Scientist Broke the Rules to Create the First Gene-Edited Babies." *The Wall Street Journal*, Dow Jones & Company, 10 May 2019, https://www.wsj.com/articles/how-a-chinese-scientist-broke-the-rules-to-create-the-first-gene-edited-babies-11557506697.

Rana, Preetika, and Wenxin Fan. "Chinese Scientist Claims World's First Genetically Modified Babies." *The Wall Street Journal*, Dow Jones & Company, 26 Nov. 2018, https://www.wsj.com/articles/chinese-scientist-claims-worlds-first-genetically-modified-babies-1543258316.

Ran, F., Hsu, P., Wright, J. *et al.* Genome engineering using the CRISPR-Cas9 system. *Nat Protoc* **8,** 2281–2308 (2013). https://doi.org/10.1038/nprot.2013.143

Dimmock, Mark. *Ethics for A-Level.* OPEN Book Publishers, 2017.

"Chinese Scientist Who Produced Genetically Altered Babies Sentenced to 3 Years in Jail." *Science*, https://www.science.org/content/article/chinese-scientist-who-produced-genetically-altered-babies-sentenced-3-years-jail.

Kidd C, Hayden BY. The Psychology and Neuroscience of Curiosity. *Neuron.* 2015;88(3):449-460. doi:10.1016/j.neuron.2015.09.010

Why?: What Makes Us Curious, Mario Livio (Author), Arthur Morey (Narrator), Simon & Schuster Audio (Publisher)

Aurelius, Marcus. *Meditations.* Blurb, 2021.

Halal Foods - Texas A&M University. http://animalscience.tamu. edu/wp-content/uploads/sites/14/2016/01/Halal-Foods.pdf.

"What Is Halal? A Guide for Non-Muslims." *Islamic Council of Victoria (ICV)*, https://www.icv.org.au/about/about-islam-overview/what-is-halal-a-guide-for-non-muslims/.

Little, Becky. "How Did Humans Evolve?" *History.com*, A&E Television Networks, 5 Mar. 2020, https://www.history.com/news/humans-evolution-neanderthals-denisovans.

Kochanek KD, Xu JQ, Arias E. Mortality in the United States, 2019. NCHS Data Brief, no 395. Hyattsville, MD: National Center for Health Statistics. 2020.

Ryrie, Charles C. Ryrie Study Bible: *New American Standard Bible*, 1995 Update. Chicago: Moody Press, 1995. Print.

"The Purpose of Life on Earth." *Mormon Beliefs*, mormonbeliefs.org/mormon_ beliefs/mormon-beliefs-the-plan-of-salvation/the-plan-of-salvation-the-purpose-of-life-on-earth/.

Posts, Related. "Purpose of Life According to Islam; Quranic Verses." *Islamic Articles*, 9 May 2019, http://www.quranreading.com/blog/purpose-of-life-according-to-islam-quranic-verses/.

"Surah Adh-Dhariyat - 56." *Quran.com*, https://quran.com/51:56 ?store=false&translations=149%2C95%2C84.

What Is Life's Purpose? - Kabbalah, Chassidism and Jewish ... https:// www.chabad.org/library/article_cdo/aid/108390/jewish/What-is-Lifes-Purpose.htm.

Hindu Beliefs - Religionfacts. https://religionfacts.com/hinduism/beliefs.

Sivakumar, Akhilesh, et al. "The Meaning of Life According to Hinduism." *Philosophy 1100H Blog*, 12 Oct. 2014, https://u.osu.edu/group5/2014/10/12/the-meaning-of-life-according-to-hinduism/comment-page-1/.

"The Four Goals of Hindu Life: Kama, Artha, Dharma & Moksha." *Study.com*, 11 March 2014, study.com/academy/lesson/the-four-goals-of-hindu-life-kama-artha-dharma-moksha.html

"What Is the Purpose of Life in Buddhism." *Teachings of the Buddha*, https://teachingsofthebuddha.com/what-is-the-purpose-of-life-in-buddhism/.

"Four Noble Truths: The Buddhist Centre." *Four Noble Truths | The Buddhist Centre*, https://thebuddhistcentre.com/text/four-noble-truths.

Speed, David, et al. "What Do You Mean, 'What Does It All Mean?' Atheism, Nonreligion, and Life Meaning." *SAGE Open*, vol. 8, no. 1, 2018, p. 215824401775423., doi:10.1177/2158244017754238.

Aristote, et al. *Aristotle's Nicomachean Ethics.* University of Chicago Press, 2011.

Fischer, Kirsten. *American Freethinker Elihu Palmer and the Struggle for Religious Freedom in the New Nation.* University of Pennsylvania Press, 2021.

Kuhn, TS. *The Structure of Scientific Revolutions.* Chicago University Press, 1970.

"The Psychology of Purpose - Discover More." *John Templeton Foundation*, 7 Aug. 2020, www.templeton.org/discoveries/the-psychology-of-purpose.

Coleman, T. J., III, & Hood, R. W., Jr. (2015). Reconsidering everything: From folk categories to existential theory of mind. [Peer commentary on the journal article "From weird experiences to revelatory events" by A. Taves]. Religion and Society: Advances in Research, 6(1), 18-22

Bering, J. (2002). The existential theory of mind. *Review of General Psychology*, 6(1), 3-24. doi:10.1037/1089-2680.6.1.3

Bering, J. (2003). Towards a cognitive theory of existential meaning. *New Ideas in Psychology*, 21, 101-120. doi:10.1016/s0732-118x(03)00014-x

Frankl, Viktor Emil, and Hse Lasch. *Man's Search for Meaning: an Introduction to Logotheraphy.* Hodder and Stoughton, 1962.

Galen, L. W. (2017a). Overlapping mental magisteria: Implications of experimental psychology for a theory of religious belief as misattribution. *Method & Theory in the Study of Religion,* 29, 221-267. doi:10.1163/15700682-12341393

Galen, L. W. (2017b). Which functions assumed to be religious and spiritual in nature are ultimately attributable or reducible to purely secular mechanisms? Religion, Brain & Behavior, 7, 293-295. doi:10.1080/2153599X.2016.1249919

Clore, Gerald L. "Psychology and the Rationality of Emotion." *Modern Theology,* vol. 27, no. 2, 2011, pp. 325–338., https://doi.org/10.1111/j.1468-0025.2010.01679.x.

Schnell, T. (2009). The Sources of Meaning and Meaning in Life Questionnaire (SoMe): Relations to demographics and well-being. *The Journal of Positive Psychology,* 4, 483-499. doi:10.1080/17439760903271074

Loewenstein, G. (1994). The psychology of curiosity: A review and reinterpretation. *Psychological Bulletin, 116*(1), 75–98. https://doi.org/10.1037/0033-2909.116.1.75

"Why Are We So Curious?" *BBC Future,* BBC, www.bbc.com/future/article/20120618-why-are-we-so-curious.

Smith, Charles Kay (1990). "A model for understanding the evolution of mammalian behavior". *Current Mammalogy.* **2**: 335–374.

Edwards, Tab. *Imperfekt.* TMBE, 2015.

Prothero, Stephen R. *God Is Not One the Eight Rival Religions That Run the World.* HarperOne, 2011.

Cochrane, Linda (2011). *Is Man a Rational Animal?* Concordia University Montreal

Kalberg, Stephen. "Max Weber's Types of Rationality: Cornerstones for the Analysis of Rationalization Processes in History." *American Journal of Sociology*, vol. 85, no. 5, 1980, pp. 1145–1179., doi:10.1086/227128.

AARP, September 3, and September 3 AARP. "AARP Joins Forces With Wish of a Lifetime." *AARP*, 3 Sept. 2020, www.aarp.org/about-aarp/info-2020/wish-of-a-lifetime.html.

"Wish Stories." *Wish of a Lifetime*, 20 Oct. 2020, wishofalifetime.org/wish-stories/.

Seneca, Lucius Annaeus. *On the Shortness of Life*. Benediction Classics, 2018.

"On the Shortness of Life: Book Summary, Key Lessons, and Best Quotes." *Daily Stoic*, 20 Mar. 2018, dailystoic.com/on-the-shortness-of-life-seneca/.

"Human Being." *Encyclopedia Britannica*, Encyclopedia Britannica, Inc., www.britannica.com/topic/human-being.

Stillman, Jessica. "Scientists Asked Hundreds of People What Advice They Would Give Their Younger Selves. Here Are the 5 Most Common Answers." *Inc.com*, Inc., 13 June 2019, www.inc.com/jessica-stillman/the-5-most-common-pieces-of-advice-people-wish-they-could-give-their-younger-selves.html.

Robin M. Kowalski & Annie McCord (2020) If I knew then what I know now: Advice to my younger self, *The Journal of Social Psychology*, 160:1, 1-20, DOI: 10.1080/00224545.2019.1609401

Svavarsdóttir, Sigrún. "The Virtue of Practical Rationality." *Philosophy and Phenomenological Research*, vol. 77, no. 1, 2008, pp. 1–33. *JSTOR*, www.jstor.org/stable/40041217. Accessed 22 July 2021.

"Oxford Languages and Google - English." *Oxford Languages*, languages.oup.com/google-dictionary-en/.

"Practical." PRACTICAL | *Definition in the Cambridge English Dictionary*, dictionary.cambridge.org/us/dictionary/english/practical.

Stone, Jim. "A Theory of Religion Revised." *Religious Studies*, vol. 37, no. 2, 2001, pp. 177–189. *JSTOR*, www.jstor.org/stable/20008342. Accessed 22 July 2021.

Internet Encyclopedia of Philosophy, iep.utm.edu/faith-re/.

Helm, Paul, ed. *Faith and Reason*. Oxford: Oxford University Press, 1999.

Halford, Graeme S et al. "Separating cognitive capacity from knowledge: a new hypothesis." *Trends in cognitive sciences* vol. 11,6 (2007): 236-42. doi:10.1016/j.tics.2007.04.001

St.B. T. Evans, Jonathan. "The Cognitive Psychology of Reasoning: An Introduction." *The Quarterly Journal of Experimental Psychology Section A*, vol. 46, no. 4, Nov. 1993, pp. 561–567, doi:10.1080/14640749308401027.

Bernstein, Jeffrey. *10 Days to a Less DEFIANT Child: The Breakthrough Program for Overcoming Your Child's Difficult Behavior*. Da Capo Life Long, a Member of the Perseus Books Group, 2015.

Warren, Rick. *The Purpose-Driven Life: What on Earth Am i Here for?* Zondervan, 2016.

Stanford Encyclopedia of Philosophy. Stanford University, Metaphysics Research Lab., 2004.

Bishop, John. "Faith." *Stanford Encyclopedia of Philosophy*, Stanford University, 30 Mar. 2016, plato.stanford.edu/entries/faith/.

"What Is Faith? -: Biblical Definition of Faith." *NIV Bible*, 28 Apr. 2021, www.thenivbible.com/blog/what-is-faith/.

Koppe, Katharina, and Klaus Rothermund. "Let It Go: Depression Facilitates Disengagement from Unattainable Goals." *Journal of Behavior Therapy and Experimental Psychiatry*, vol. 54, 2017, pp. 278–284., doi:10.1016/j.jbtep.2016.10.003.

"Letting Go of Unattainable Goals Has Psychological Perks." *Psychology Today*, Sussex Publishers, www.psychologytoday.com/us/blog/the-athletes-way/201702/letting-go-unattainable-goals-has-psychological-perks.

"In Search of Myths & Heroes. Shangri-La." *PBS*, Public Broadcasting Service, www.pbs.org/mythsandheroes/myths_four_shangrila.html.

Wood, Michael. *In Search of Myths & Heroes: EXPLORING Four Epic Legends of the World*. University of California Press, 2005.

Brahm, Laurence, director. *Searching for Shangri-La*. You-Tube, Shambhala Studio, 1 July 2016, www.youtube.com/watch?v=wLkm8UFWCyo.

Metz, Thaddeus (2013). *Meaning in life*. Oxford: Oxford University Press. ISBN 978-0-19-959931-8.

Tolstoy, Leo. *A Confession*. Dover, 2005.

"An Analysis of the Meaning of Life as Mentioned by Socrates via the Soul Centered Theory." *Kibin*, www.kibin.com/essay-examples/an-analysis-of-the-meaning-of-life-as-mentioned-by-socrates-via-the-soul-centered-theory-H0CvKhXF.

Grayling, A.C. "Socrates and the Meaning of Life." *The Meaning of Life and the Great Philosophers*, 2018, pp. 27–32., doi:10.4324/9781315385945-4.

Cope, Em. *Platos Phaedo*. Scholars Choice, 2015.

Reker, G.T., & Wong, P.T.P. (1988). "Aging as an individual process: Towards a theory of personal meaning." In J.E. Birren, & V.L. Bengston (Eds.), *Emergent theories of aging* (pp. 214–246). New York: Springer.

Wong, P. T. P. (2010). The PURE strategy to create lean and excellent organizations. *International Journal of Existential Psychology and Psychotherapy, 3*(2), 1-21.

Korsgaard, Christine M. "Aristotle's Function Argument." *The Constitution of Agency*, 2008, pp. 129–150., doi:10.1093/acprof:oso/9780199552733.003.0005.

Metz, Thaddeus, "The Meaning of Life", *The Stanford Encyclopedia of Philosophy* (Spring 2021 Edition), Edward N. Zalta (ed.), URL = <https://plato.stanford.edu/archives/spr2021/entries/life-meaning/>.

Pratt, Alan. "Nihilism." *Internet Encyclopedia of Philosophy*, iep. utm.edu/nihilism/.

Ross, W. D. *Plato's Theory of Ideas*. Greenwood Press, 1976.

Curzer, Howard J. *Aristotle and the Virtues*. Oxford University Press, 2015.

Jepkemboi G. (2018) The Effects of Hunger on Physical and Cognitive Development of Children. In: Szente J. (eds) Assisting Young Children Caught in Disasters. Educating the Young Child (Advances in Theory and Research, Implications for Practice), vol 13. Springer, Cham. https://doi.org/10.1007/978-3-319-62887-5_10

Pruitt, Derek. "Effects of Starvation on Adults and Children." *Backpack Buddies Foundation of Loudoun*, Backpack Buddies Foundation of Loudoun, 9 Aug. 2020, https://www.bbfloudoun.org/news/2019/5/2/effects-of-starvation-on-adults-and-children.

Casabianca, Sandra Silva. "Feeling Empty? Here's What It Could Mean and How to Stop It." *Psych Central*, Psych Central, 29 Mar. 2021, https://psychcentral.com/blog/stop-feeling-empty#feeling-empty-all-the-time.

Sarah Lewis, PharmD. "Kenophobia (Fear of Empty Spaces): Causes, Symptoms & Treatments." *Healthgrades*, Healthgrades, 16 Oct. 2020, https://www.healthgrades.com/right-care/anxiety-disorders/kenophobia-fear-of-empty-spaces.

"Declaring Moral Bankruptcy." *Psychology Today*, Sussex Publishers, https://www.psychologytoday.com/us/blog/philosophy-stirred-not-shaken/201410/declaring-moral-bankruptcy.

"Counseling Center." *University of North Carolina Wilmington*, https://uncw.edu/counseling/selfworth.html.

Park, Lora E., et al. "Attachment Styles and Contingencies of Self-Worth." *Personality and Social Psychology Bulletin*, vol. 30, no. 10, 2004, pp. 1243–1254., https://doi.org/10.1177/0146167204264000.

Maslow, A. H. (1943). A theory of human motivation. *Psychological Review, 50*(4), 370–396. https://doi.org/10.1037/h0054346

Boxrec: Sonny Liston. https://boxrec.com/en/proboxer/9031.

https://positivepsychology.com/self-worth/

"30 Of Muhammad Ali's Best Quotes." *USA Today*, Gannett Satellite Information Network, 5 June 2016, https://www.usatoday.com/story/sports/boxing/2016/06/03/muhammad-ali-best-quotes-boxing/85370850/.

Primack, Brian A., et al. "Social Media Use and Perceived Social Isolation among Young Adults in the U.S." *American Journal of Preventive Medicine*, vol. 53, no. 1, 2017, pp. 1–8., https://doi.org/10.1016/j.amepre.2017.01.010.

Crocker, J., & Luhtanen, R. K. (2003). Level of self-esteem and contingencies of self-worth: Unique effects on academic, social, and financial problems in college freshmen. *Personality and Social Psychology Bulletin*, 29, 701-712.

Crocker, J., Luhtanen, R. K., Cooper, M. L., & Bouvrette, A. (2003). Contingencies of self-worth in college students: Theory and measurement. *Journal of Personality and Social Psychology*, 85, 894-908.

M.D., Fredric. "Low Self-esteem." Psychology Today. Accessed March 3, 2014. http://www.psychologytoday.com/blog/fighting-fear/201304/low-self-esteem

Reuters. "'I Am the Greatest:' Muhammad Ali in His Own Words." *Newsweek*, Newsweek, 17 June 2016, https://www.newsweek.com/i-am-greatest-muhammad-ali-own-words-466432.

BlackPast, contributed by: "(1982) Audre Lorde, 'Learning from the 60s' •." *(1982) Audre Lorde, "Learning from the 60s"* •, 24 Sept. 2019, https://www.blackpast.org/african-american-history/1982-audre-lorde-learning-60s/.

"Looking after Yourself." *CCI*, https://www.cci.health.wa.gov.au/Resources/Looking-After-Yourself.

Alton, Larry. "Why Low Self-Esteem May Be Hurting You at Work." *NBCNews.com*, NBCUniversal News Group, 13 Apr. 2018, https://www.nbcnews.com/better/amp/ncna814156.

Nguyen, Dat Tan, et al. "Low Self-Esteem and Its Association with Anxiety, Depression, and Suicidal Ideation in Vietnamese Secondary School Students: A Cross-Sectional Study." *Frontiers in Psychiatry*, vol. 10, 2019, https://doi.org/10.3389/fpsyt.2019.00698.

Article: "Self-Esteem Development From Young Adulthood to Old Age: A Cohort-Sequential Longitudinal Study,» Ulrich Orth, PhD, University of Basel, Kali H. Trzesniewski, PhD, University of Western Ontario and Richard W. Robins, PhD, University of California, Davis; *Journal of Personality and Social Psychology*, Vol. 98, No. 4.

"Self-Esteem Declines Sharply among Older Adults While Middle-Aged Are Most Confident." *American Psychological Association*, American Psychological Association, https://www.apa.org/news/press/releases/2010/04/self-esteem.

McClure, Auden C., et al. "Characteristics Associated with Low Self-Esteem among Us Adolescents." *Academic Pediatrics*, vol. 10, no. 4, 2010, https://doi.org/10.1016/j.acap.2010.03.007.

Real Girls, Real Pressure: A National Report om the State of Self-Esteem

McCall, G. J., & Simmons, J. L. (1978). Identities and interactions (Rev. ed.). New York, NY: Free Press.

Stets, Jan E., and Peter J. Burke. "Identity Theory and Social Identity Theory." *Social Psychology Quarterly* 63, no. 3 (2000): 224–37. https://doi.org/10.2307/2695870.

American Psychological Association. (2010, April 1). *Self-esteem declines sharply among older adults while middle-aged are most confident* [Press release]. http://www.apa.org/news/press/releases/2010/04/self-esteem

Greenwald, Anthony G., et al. "Consequential Validity of the Implicit Association Test: Comment on Blanton and Jaccard (2006)." *American Psychologist*, vol. 61, no. 1, 2006, pp. 56–61., https://doi.org/10.1037/0003-066x.61.1.56.

Zimmerman, Michael J. and Ben Bradley, "Intrinsic vs. Extrinsic Value", *The Stanford Encyclopedia of Philosophy* (Spring 2019 Edition), Edward N. Zalta (ed.), URL = <https://plato.stanford.edu/archives/spr2019/entries/value-intrinsic-extrinsic/>.

"Primitive Society." *Primitive Society - an Overview | ScienceDirect Topics*, https://www.sciencedirect.com/topics/social-sciences/primitive-society.

M. Becker, V. L. Vignoles, E. Owe, M. J. Easterbrook, R. Brown, P. B. Smith, M. H. Bond, C. Regalia, C. Manzi, M. Brambilla, S. Aldhafri, R. Gonzalez, D. Carrasco, M. Paz Cadena, S. Lay, I. Schweiger Gallo, A. Torres, L. Camino, E. Ozgen, U. E. Guner, N. Yamako lu, F. C. Silveira Lemos, E. V. Trujillo, P. Balanta, M. E. J. Macapagal, M. Cristina Ferreira, G. Herman, I. de Sauvage, D. Bourguignon, Q. Wang, M. Fulop, C. Harb, A. Chybicka, K. H. Mekonnen, M. Martin, G. Nizharadze, A. Gavreliuc, J. Buitendach, A. Valk, S. H. Koller. Cultural Bases for Self-Evaluation: Seeing Oneself Positively in Different Cultural Contexts. *Personality and Social Psychology Bulletin*, 2014; DOI: 10.1177/0146167214522836

"Self-Esteem Declines Sharply among Older Adults While Middle-Aged Are Most Confident." *American Psychological Association*, American Psychological Association, https://www.apa.org/news/press/releases/2010/04/self-esteem.

Margarita Tartakovsky, MS. "When You Feel Worthless." *Psych Central*, Psych Central, 2 Sept. 2014, https://psychcentral.com/blog/when-you-feel-worthless#1.

Kotecki, Peter. "9 Useless Body Parts That Humans No Longer Need." *Business Insider*, Business Insider, 16 Jan. 2019, https://www.businessinsider.com/human-useless-body-parts-2019-1.

Nelson, Michael, "Existence", *The Stanford Encyclopedia of Philosophy* (Summer 2020 Edition), Edward N. Zalta (ed.), URL = <https://plato.stanford.edu/archives/sum2020/entries/existence/>.

Sherman, Audrey. "Characteristics of High and Low Self-Esteem." *PsychSkills*, 28 May 2020, https://psychskills.com/characteristics-of-high-and-low-self-esteem/.

Overcoming the Need to Please | Psychology Today. https://www.psychologytoday.com/us/blog/nurturing-self-compassion/201710/overcoming-the-need-please.

Heslin, Rachel S. *Navigating Life: 8 Different Strategies to Guide Your Way*. Createspace Independent P, 2017.

Why Do We Constantly Seek the Approval of Others ... https://www.psychologytoday.com/us/blog/working-through-shame/201906/why-do-we-constantly-seek-the-approval-others.

Sweeney, T. J. (1989). *Adlerian counseling: A practical approach for a new decade (3rd ed)*.

Muncie, IN: Accelerated Development.

Griffith, Jane, and Robert L. Powers. *The Lexicon of Adlerian Psychology: 106 Terms Associated with the Individual Psychology of Alfred Adler*. Adlerian Psychology Associates, 2007.

"Apa Dictionary of Psychology." *American Psychological Association*, American Psychological Association, https://dictionary.apa.org/psychological-need.

SoP, et al. "Basic Psychological Needs." *The Science of Psychotherapy*, 5 Apr. 2021, https://www.thescienceofpsychotherapy.com/basic-psychological-needs/.

SoP. "Consistency Theory." *The Science of Psychotherapy*, 1 Oct. 2018, https://www.thescienceofpsychotherapy.com/glossary/consistency-theory/.

Grawe, K. (2004). *Psychological therapy*. Toronto: Hogrefe & Huber.

Grawe, K. (2007). *Neuropsychotherapy: How the Neurosciences Inform Effective Psychotherapy* (1st ed.). Routledge.

Sendhil Mullainathan and Eldar Shafir, *Scarcity: The New Science of Having Less and How It Defines Our Lives* (New York: Times Books, 2013).

"Scarcity: Why Having Too Little Means so Much by Sendhil Mullainathan and Eldar Shafir – Review." *The Guardian*, Guardian News and Media, 7 Sept. 2013, https://www.theguardian.com/books/2013/sep/07/scarcity-sendhil-mullainathan-shafir-review.

"Respect." *RESPECT | Definition in the Cambridge English Dictionary*, https://dictionary.cambridge.org/us/dictionary/english/respect.

"Six Fundamental Human Needs We Need to Meet to Live Our Best Lives." *Forbes*, Forbes Magazine, 10 Dec. 2021, https://www.forbes.com/sites/quora/2018/02/05/six-fundamental-human-needs-we-need-to-meet-to-live-our-best-lives/?sh=432adb82344a.

Thomson, William Archibald Robson, Richardson, Robert G., Guthrie, Douglas James, Rhodes, Philip and Underwood, E. Ashworth. "History of medicine". *Encyclopedia Britannica*, 27 Aug. 2020, https://www.britannica.com/science/history-of-medicine. Accessed 6 February 2022.

Common cold. Centers for Disease Control and Prevention. https://www.cdc.gov/antibiotic-use/community/for-patients/common-illnesses/colds.html. Accessed Jan. 15, 2021.

"Common Cold." *Mayo Clinic*, Mayo Foundation for Medical Education and Research, 11 June 2021, https://www.mayoclinic.org/diseases-conditions/common-cold/symptoms-causes/syc-20351605?utm_source=Google&utm_medium=abstract&utm_content=Common-cold&utm_campaign=Knowledge-panel.

"Overcome The 5 Main Reasons People Resist Change." *Forbes.* Forbes Magazine, 26 Nov. 2012. 02 Nov. 2014. <http://www. forbes.com/sites/lisaquast/2012/11/26/overcome-the-5-main-reasons-people-resist-change/>

Henriques, Gregg. *A New Unified Theory of Psychology.* Springer, 2011.

Deci, E. L., & Ryan, R. M. (2012). Self-determination theory. In P. A. M. Van Lange, A. W. Kruglanski, & E. T. Higgins (Eds.), *Handbook of theories of social psychology* (pp. 416–436). Sage Publications Ltd. https://doi.org/10.4135/9781446249215.n21

Davion, Victoria. "Competition, Recognition, and Approval-Seeking." *Hypatia*, vol. 3, no. 2, [Hypatia, Inc., Wiley], 1988, pp. 165–66, http://www.jstor.org/stable/3809962.

Healthy Sense of Self. "Who Cares What They Think: Overcome Approval-Seeking Behavior." *Healthy Sense of Self*, 19 Sept. 2019, https://healthysenseofself.com/release-approval-addiction/.

Jones E. E., Gergen, K., & Davis, K. Some reactions to being approved or disapproved as a person. Psychological Monographs, 1962, 76(Whole No. 521).

O., J. L. "Desperately Seeking Validation." *Medium*, Change Becomes You, 8 Mar. 2022, https://medium.com/change-becomes-you/desperately-seeking-validation-238f1db7c25c.

Winch, Guy. *Emotional First Aid: Healing Rejection, Guilt, Failure, and Other Everyday Hurts.* Plume, 2014.

"Deadwood, SD." *Data USA*, https://datausa.io/profile/ geo/deadwood-sd#:~:text=Median%20Household%20 Income,-%2444%2C871&text=Households%20in%20 Deadwood%2C%20SD%20have,represents%20a%20 7.06%25%20annual%20growth.

Wire, SI. "Griner Said She Could Beat Cousins One-on-One." *Sports Illustrated*, Sports Illustrated, 17 Aug. 2016, https:// www.si.com/olympics/2016/08/17/brittney-griner-demarcus-cousins-one-on-one-challenge#:~:text=Last%20week%2C%20

Griner%20told%20USA,taunting%20the%20Sacrementio%20
Kings%20center.&text=%E2%80%9CI'm%20glad%20she's%20
that,little%20delusional%E2%80%9D%20Cousins%20told%20
ESPN.

Amick, Sam. "Rio Olympic Trashtalking: Brittney Griner
Wants Shot at DeMarcus Cousins." *USA Today*, Gannett
Satellite Information Network, 10 Aug. 2016, https://www.
usatoday.com/story/sports/olympics/rio-2016/2016/08/09/
basketball-team-usa-trashtalking-brittney-griner-demarcus-
cousins/88493350/.

Wood, Terry M. *Measurement in Physical Education and Exercise
Science: Measurement, Statistics and Research Design in Physical Ed-
ucation and Exercise Science; Current Issues and Trends.* Lawrence
Erlbaum, 1997.

"How Bad Is Lying: The Psychology behind Lies." *Psytherapy*,
25 Mar. 2019, https://psytherapy.co.uk/why-do-we-lie/.

DePaulo, B. M., Kashy, D. A., Kirkendol, S. E., Wyer, M. M., &
Epstein, J. A. (1996). Lying in everyday life. *Journal of Personality and Social Psychology*, 70(5), 979–995. doi: 10.1037/0022-
3514.70.5.979

Zuckerman, M., DePaulo, B. M., & Rosenthal, R. (1981). Verbal and nonverbal communication of deception. In *Advances
in experimental social psychology*, 14, 1-59. Academic Press.

The Costs of Lying: Consequences of ... - Essay.utwente.nl. https://es-
say.utwente.nl/85697/1/Preuter_MA_Psychology.pdf.

"The Real Reason We Look for Validation and Approval...and
How to Overcome It." *Karengeddis.com*, 13 Dec. 2020, http://
karengeddis.com/why-we-look-for-validation.

"Prestige (Sociology)." *Psychology Wiki*, https://psychology.fan-
dom.com/wiki/Prestige_(sociology).

Delgado, Jennifer. "People Who Brag a Lot Need to Fill Gaps
in Their Identity." *Psychology Spot*, Jennifer Delgado Suárez,
7 Oct. 2019, https://psychology-spot.com/people-who-brag/.

Wicklund, R. A. & Gollwitzer, P. M. (1981) Symbolic Self-Completion, Attempted Influence, and Self-Deprecation. *Basic and Applied Social Psychology; 2 (2): 89-114.*

J. Dickler. "Being Rich May Increase Your Odds of Divorce." *CNBC*, CNBC, 10 Oct. 2018, https://www.cnbc.com/2018/10/10/being-rich-may-increase-your-odds-of-divorce.html.

Crecca, Carrie, et al. "Wondering How Much to Spend on an Engagement Ring? Here's Why Natural Diamonds Are the Best Investment." *Only Natural Diamonds*, 22 Dec. 2021, https://www.naturaldiamonds.com/love-diamonds-romance-symbolism/whats-the-price-of-love-a-guide-on-what-to-spend-on-an-engagement-ring/?gclid=Cj0KCQ-iA3rKQBhCNARIsACUEW_Z9aKKSHlpfMX_j9_kc3HI-hE1hjai2kkYxKL9PabDBxI8xpOFt3RxkaAnfoEALw_wcB&gclsrc=aw.ds.

Montemayor, Cristina. "How to Propose without a Ring." *Brides*, Brides, 5 Feb. 2022, https://www.brides.com/story/proposal-without-a-ring-real-brides-share#:~:text=Although%20it's%20tradition%20to%20propose,would%20wear%20or%20enjoy%20more.&text=It's%20not%20the%20ring%20that,the%20rest%20of%20your%20lives.

Staff, Us Weekly. "The 10 Most Expensive Celebrity Engagement Rings of All Time." *Us Weekly*, 13 Apr. 2021, https://www.usmagazine.com/stylish/pictures/most-expensive-celebrity-engagement-rings-of-all-time-pics/kim-kardashian-124/.

Hanson, Chiaku. "Why Are Women so Insecure?" *HuffPost*, HuffPost, 1 Mar. 2017, https://www.huffpost.com/entry/why-are-women-so-insecure_b_9352540.

"D.B. Cooper Hijacking." *FBI*, FBI, 18 May 2016, https://www.fbi.gov/history/famous-cases/db-cooper-hijacking.

Greenwood, Dara, et al. "Fame and the Social Self: The Need to Belong, Narcissism, and Relatedness Predict the Appeal of Fame." *Personality and Individual Differences*, vol. 55, no. 5, 2013, pp. 490–495., https://doi.org/10.1016/j.paid.2013.04.020.

Baumeister, R. F., & Leary, M. R. (1995). The need to belong: Desire for interpersonal attachments as a fundamental human motivation. *Psychological Bulletin*, 117, 497–529.

Deci, E. L., & Ryan's, R. M. (2000). The 'what' and 'why' of goal pursuits: Human needs and the self-determination of behavior. *Psychological Inquiry*, 11, 227–268.

"Narcissism and What's underneath, Part II: Admiration and Love." *Mental Help Narcissism And Whats Underneath Part II Admiration and Love Comments*, https://www.mentalhelp.net/blogs/narcissism-and-what-s-underneath-part-ii-admiration-and-love/.

Baumann, Nick. "I Am the Best: A Prose Poem by Donald J. Trump." *HuffPost*, HuffPost, 19 Dec. 2016, https://www.huffpost.com/entry/donald-trump-best-most-only_n_56f0a08ee4b03a640a6b7380.

Monica T. Whitty, Siobhan E. Carville, "Would I lie to you? Self-serving lies and other-oriented lies told across different media," *Computers in Human Behavior*, Volume 24, Issue 3, 2008, Pages 1021-1031, ISSN 0747-5632, https://doi.org/10.1016/j.chb.2007.03.004.

DePaulo, Bella & Kashy, Deborah & Kirkendol, Susan & Wyer, Melissa & Epstein, Jennifer. (1996). Lying in Everyday Life. *Journal of personality and social psychology*. 70. 979-95. 10.1037/0022-3514.70.5.979.

"Paulina Porizkova." *Wikipedia*, Wikimedia Foundation, 26 Jan. 2022, https://en.wikipedia.org/wiki/Paulina_Porizkova.

Goldman, Tom. "Dear John McEnroe: Putting Serena Williams on the Men's Circuit Is a Losing Game." *NPR*, NPR, 27 June 2017, https://www.npr.org/2017/06/27/534571590/dear-john-mcenroe-putting-serena-williams-on-the-mens-circuit-is-a-losing-game.

"'Battle of the Sexes.'" *History.com*, A&E Television Networks, 24 Nov. 2009, https://www.history.com/this-day-in-history/king-triumphs-in-battle-of-sexes.

Maglio, Tony. "Serena Williams: Andy Murray Would Beat Me 6-0, 6-0 in 5 Minutes (Video)." *TheWrap*, 23 Aug. 2013, https://www.thewrap.com/serena-williams-andy-murray-would-beat-me-6-0-6-0-5-minutes-video-112836/.

Darwall, Stephen L. "Two Kinds of Respect." *Ethics*, vol. 88, no. 1, 1977, pp. 36–49., https://doi.org/10.1086/292054.

Huo, Yuen J., and Kevin R. Binning. "Why the Psychological Experience of Respect Matters in Group Life: An Integrative Account." *Social and Personality Psychology Compass*, vol. 2, no. 4, 2008, pp. 1570–1585., https://doi.org/10.1111/j.1751-9004.2008.00129.x.

Sparknotes, SparkNotes, https://www.sparknotes.com/nofear/shakespeare/hamlet/page_230/.

Capellanus, Andreas, and John Jay Parry. *The Art of Courtly Love*. Frederick Ungar, 1959.

Pelz, Professor Bill. "Developmental Psychology." *Types of Love | Developmental Psychology*, https://courses.lumenlearning.com/suny-hccc-ss-152-1/chapter/types-of-love/.

Sternberg, R. J. (1988) *The Triangle of Love: Intimacy, Passion, Commitment*, Basic Books (ISBN 0465087469)...la:triangulus amoris

"[Solved] What Does the Deprivation of Meaningful Human Touch Do to a Person?: Course Hero." *[Solved] What Does the Deprivation of Meaningful Human Touch Do to a Person? | Course Hero*, https://www.coursehero.com/tutors-problems/Criminal-Justice/29046995-What-does-the-deprivation-of-meaningful-human-touch-do-to-a-person/.

"What Lack of Affection Can Do to You." *Psychology Today*, Sussex Publishers, https://www.psychologytoday.com/us/blog/affectionado/201308/what-lack-affection-can-do-you.

"Skin Hunger." *The University of Edinburgh*, 7 July 1970, https://www.ed.ac.uk/chaplaincy/blogs-podcasts-and-reflections/for-times-like-these/skin-hunger#:~:text='Skin%20hunger%20is%20the%20biological,as%20they%20desire%20their%20liberty.

"Who Cheats More? the Demographics of Infidelity in America." *Institute for Family Studies*, https://ifstudies.org/blog/who-cheats-more-the-demographics-of-cheating-in-america.

"Michael Bohley, MD." *Dr Michael Bohley MD*, https://www.drbohley.com/a-brief-history-of-breast-implants/.

Cook, R. R., and L. L. Perkins. "The Prevalence of Breast Implants among Women in the United States." *Current Topics in Microbiology and Immunology*, 1996, pp. 419–425., https://doi.org/10.1007/978-3-642-85226-8_45.

2020 Plastic Surgery Statistics Report. https://www.plasticsurgery.org/documents/News/Statistics/2020/plastic-surgery-statistics-report-2020.pdf.

Koff, E., Benavage, A. Breast Size Perception and Satisfaction, Body Image, and Psychological Functioning in Caucasian and Asian American College Women. *Sex Roles* **38**, 655–673 (1998). https://doi.org/10.1023/A:1018802928210

Spencer, Linda, et al. "The Relationship between Breast Size and Aspects of Health and Psychological Wellbeing in Mature-Aged Women." *Women's Health*, vol. 16, 2020, p. 174550652091833., https://doi.org/10.1177/1745506520918335.

Baggett, Catherine, et al. "Don't Objectify Me!: Sexual Self-Monitoring, Coping, and Psychological Maladjustment." *Psycho-Social Aspects of Human Sexuality and Ethics*, 2021, https://doi.org/10.5772/intechopen.90997.

Bauer, Alex. "'Basquiat' and the Art of the Biopic." *Medium*, Medium, 14 Sept. 2018, https://ambauer93.medium.com/basquiat-and-the-art-of-the-biopic-a3fe8c0488f5.

Cuncic, Arlin. "The Psychology of Racism." *Verywell Mind*, Verywell Mind, 2 Feb. 2022, https://www.verywellmind.com/the-psychology-of-racism-5070459.

Roberts S, Rizzo M. The psychology of American racism. *American Psychologist*. 2020. doi:10.1037/amp0000642

Kendi, Ibram X. *How to Be an Antiracist*. Vintage, 2021.

Sociology of Racism - Harvard University. https://scholar.harvard. edu/files/matthewclair/files/sociology_of_racism_clairandenis_2015.pdf.

"White Supremacy and Privilege: Legacies of Slavery." *Yale University Press Blog*, 12 Nov. 2019, https://blog.yalebooks. com/2019/11/22/white-supremacy-and-privilege-legacies-of-slavery/.

Segregation, Freedom's Story, TeacherServe®, National Humanities Center, http://nationalhumanitiescenter.org/tserve/freedom/1865-1917/essays/segregation.htm.

Goodell, William. *The American Slave Code in Theory and Practice: Its Distinctive Features Shown by the Statutes, Judicial Decisions, and Illustrative Facts.* Amer. and Foreign Anti-Slavery Soc., 1853.

Guy-Uriel E. Charles and Luis Fuentes-Rohwer, et al. "Pathological Racism, Chronic Racism & Targeted Universalism." *California Law Review*, 20 June 2021, https://www.californialawreview.org/print/pathological-racism-chronic-racism-targeted-universalism/#clr-toc-heading-3.

Tharps, Lori. "Selling Your House While Black: Sadly, It's a Thing." *My American Meltingpot*, 20 May 2019, https://my-americanmeltingpot.com/2019/04/29/selling-house-black-tax-real-estate/.

"Power in America." *Who Rules America: Wealth, Income, and Power*, https://whorulesamerica.ucsc.edu/power/wealth.html.

Lukes, S. (2005). *Power: A Radical View* (Second ed.). New York: Palgrave.

"The Pope and the Role of the Papacy - God and Authority in the Catholic Church - GCSE Religious Studies Revision - Edexcel - BBC Bitesize." *BBC News*, BBC, https://www.bbc.co.uk/bitesize/guides/zk8bcj6/revision/6.

"Social Dominance Explained Part I." *Psychology Today*, Sussex Publishers, https://www.psychologytoday.com/gb/blog/games-primates-play/201203/social-dominance-explained-part-i.

Articles, http://www.meaning.ca/archives/archive/art_buddhist-humility_C_Yu_Hsi.htm#1.

William James, *The Varieties of Religious Experience*. New York: Random House,1994.

"Stages of Change." *Cancer Prevention Research Center*, https://web.uri.edu/cprc/transtheoretical-model/stages-of-change/.

"Why Is It so Hard to Admit When We Are Wrong?" *Psychology Today*, Sussex Publishers, https://www.psychologytoday.com/us/blog/tech-happy-life/202101/why-is-it-so-hard-admit-when-we-are-wrong.

"The Mindset That Makes It Hard to Admit You're Wrong." *Psychology Today*, Sussex Publishers, https://www.psychology-today.com/us/blog/fulfillment-any-age/201703/the-mindset-makes-it-hard-admit-youre-wrong.

Lewicki, R. J., Polin, B., & Lount, R. J. (2016). An exploration of the structure of effective apologies. *Negotiation and Conflict Management Research, 9*(2), 177-196. doi:10.1111/ncmr.12073

Wong, Kristin. "Why It's so Hard to Admit You're Wrong." *The New York Times*, The New York Times, 22 May 2017, https://www.nytimes.com/2017/05/22/smarter-living/why-its-so-hard-to-admit-youre-wrong.html.

McLeod], [Saul. "[Cognitive Dissonance]." *Theory | Simply Psychology*, 1 Jan. 1970, https://www.simplypsychology.org/cognitive-dissonance.html.

"Respect Matters More than Money for Happiness in Life." *Association for Psychological Science - APS*, 20 June 2012, https://www.psychologicalscience.org/news/releases/respect-from-friends-matters-more-than-money-for-happiness-in-life.html.

Anderson, Cameron, et al. "The Local-Ladder Effect: Social Status and Subjective Well-Being." *Psychological Science*, vol. 23, no. 7, 2012, pp. 764–771., https://doi.org/10.1177/0956797611434537.

The Ideal of Self-Fulfillment - Princeton University. http://assets. press.princeton.edu/chapters/s6413.pdf.

"Chapter 1. the Ideal of Self-Fulfillment." *Self-Fulfillment*, 2009, pp. 3–18., https://doi.org/10.1515/9781400822744.3.

Gewirth, Alan. *Self-Fulfillment*. Princeton University Press, 2001.

Aristotle. 1941. Metaphysics 982b12-23. In The Basic Works of Aristotle. McKeon, R. ed., W. Ross, trans. New York: Random House.

Oakes, M. *I.1 What Is Philosophy - Winthrop University.* https:// faculty.winthrop.edu/oakesm/PHIL101/Web1/lessons/I.1_ What_is_Philosophy.pdf.

Halverson, W. 1967. A Concise Introduction to Philosophy. New York: Random House.

"What Is Ministering?" *The Church of Jesus Christ of Latter-Day Saints*, https://www.churchofjesuschrist.org/ministering/ what-is-ministering?lang=eng.

Walker, Harriet. "Paulina Porizkova: The Supermodel Who Dared to Look Her Age." *Times2 | The Times*, The Times, 9 Jan. 2022, https://www.thetimes.co.uk/article/paulina-poriz-kova-the-supermodel-who-dared-to-look-her-age-nfhz8c6kn.

C Szedlak, M. J. Smith, B. Callary. (2021) Developing a 'letter to my younger self' to learn from the experiences of expert coaches. *Qualitative Research in Sport, Exercise and Health* 13:4, pages 569-585.

Bunge, Jacob, and Jesse Newman. "To Stay on the Land, American Farmers Add Extra Jobs." *The Wall Street Journal*, Dow Jones & Company, 25 Feb. 2018, https://www.wsj. com/articles/to-stay-on-the-land-american-farmers-add-extra-jobs-1519582071.

Kruglanski AW, Szumowska E. Habitual Behavior Is Goal-Driven. *Perspectives on Psychological Science.* 2020;15(5):1256-1271. doi:10.1177/1745691620917676

Hangst, Andrea. "Cowboys Rookie Randy Gregory: 'I'm Immature,'" Denies Having a 'Weed Problem.'" *Sportsnaut*, 5 May 2015, https://sportsnaut.com/cowboys-rookie-randy-gregory-im-immature-denies-having-a-weed-problem/.

Le Penne, S. Longing to Belong: Needing to be Needed in a World in Need. *Soc* 54, 535–536 (2017). https://doi.org/10.1007/s12115-017-0185-y

Falzone, Diana. "Insta-Hookers? Sites Say They Expose 'Instagram Models' Who Are Really Prostitutes." *Fox News*, FOX News Network, 19 July 2016, https://www.foxnews.com/entertainment/insta-hookers-sites-say-they-expose-instagram-models-who-are-really-prostitutes.

www.ingramcontent.com/pod-product-compliance
Lightning Source LLC
Chambersburg PA
CBHW030150310326
41914CB00099B/1799/J